MANCHESTER
THE HIDDEN HISTORY

MANCHESTER

THE HIDDEN HISTORY

MICHAEL NEVELL

First published 2008

The History Press Ltd
The Mill, Brimscombe Port
Stroud, Gloucestershire, GL5 2QG
www.thehistorypress.co.uk

British Library Cataloguing in Publication Data.
A catalogue record for this book is available from the British Library.

ISBN 978 0 7524 4704 9

Typesetting and origination by The History Press Ltd.
Printed in Great Britain

CONTENTS

ACKNOWLEDGEMENTS

This volume is based on the work and knowledge of many local archaeologists and historians. More people than ever are now studying Manchester's past, whether it be post-graduate students, professional archaeologists and historians, members of local societies or Manchester school children. Much of the recent fieldwork has been undertaken by the staff of the University of Manchester Archaeology Unit and I would like to thank the following past and present members of UMAU for their continued enthusiasm in recovering Manchester's past: Dr Peter Arrowsmith, Simon Askew, Steve Bell, Peter Connelly, Phil Cooke, Ruth Garrett, Dr Richard Gregory, Lee Gregory, Brian Grimsditch, David Lloyd, Graham Mottershead, Peter Noble, John Roberts, David Power, Adam Thompson, Philip Wilson and Joanna Wright.

The inspiration for much of this work lies in the background research undertaken for Manchester's World Heritage Site bid; I would like to thank English Heritage for commissioning that work and Prof. Alan Kidd, Dr Terry Wyke, Robina McNeil and Claire Hartwell for the lively debates and hard work that the project involved, from which this book has ultimately benefited. Many other individuals have helped with advice and detailed information, particularly the professional archaeologists from the many units which now work within the city. I would like to thank them for access to their sites and works, but in particular Ian Miller of Oxford Archaeology North and John Walker of the York Archeological Trust for the many opportunities to discuss a number of subjects which appear in this work. I am also extremely grateful to Bernard and Jill Champness, Norman Redhead and in particular to Catherine Nevell for taking time to read drafts of chapters and for making many suggestions that have undoubtedly improved the final text.

My wife Catherine has borne the brunt of both my research and writing for many years, along with the chaos that has followed in its wake; her assistance, constant support and encouragement are enormously appreciated.

Finally, I dedicate this book to the memory of two friends who worked tirelessly to research and promote Manchester's archaeology – Professor Barri Jones (1936-99) and Robina McNeil (1950-2007).

CHAPTER 1

INTRODUCTION

Manchester was, and perhaps still is, a controversial city. It was described around 1540 by the antiquarian John Leland in almost idyllic terms as the 'the fairest, best buildid, quickest and populus tounne of al Lancastreshire'. Visitors in the late seventeen and eighteenth centuries commented upon the town's lack of government, its domestic-based industry and the great increase in its streets and buildings. Those viewing the city in the nineteenth century were astounded or, like the social and political commentator Frederick Engels, more of 10 horrified by the city's industrial face, the hundreds of cotton factories and chimneys, the narrow alleyways and over-crowded houses, most of which were packed into the present twenty-first-century city centre. The city was prominent in Victorian literature and was the inspiration for novels by amongst others Charles Dickens (*Hard Times*) and Elizabeth Gaskell (*Mary Barton*), books designed to raise awareness about the social injustices of industrialisation and the factory system. The 'Manchester school of economics', a term coined by the Victorian prime minister and novelist Benjamin Disraeli, with at its heart the idea of Free Trade, had a significant impact on Victorian and Edwardian economic and political life. In the twentieth century Manchester became known as a symbol of industrial decline and latterly as a renewed, regenerated city and a cultural centre, the home of the Hacienda nightclub and two of the nation's sporting giants, Manchester United football club and the Lancashire Cricket Club. Manchester was famous and controversial because of its success or excess, depending upon your point of view, in industry and popular culture.

What has this to do with archaeology? After all, archaeologists work with material culture, bricks, pottery, glass; the physical remains of the past. Yet to undertake archaeological excavation or the historic recording of a building within modern Manchester is also a matter of excavating these past impressions of the city, which still influence the outlook of modern twenty-first-century Manchester.

THE DEVELOPMENT OF ARCHAEOLOGICAL INTEREST IN MANCHESTER

There is a long tradition of archaeological study and investigation within the City of Manchester. From the 1880s the University of Manchester has been at the forefront of this research, through the work of a succession of lecturers in history and curators based within the Manchester Museum, and, from 1969, through the Archaeology Department. The Deansgate Dig of 1972, which explored the Roman settlement to the north of the fort, was an important moment in the development of modern archaeological research within the city (1). Not only did it demonstrate the survival of Roman and nineteenth-century archaeology deposits within the city centre, just a few centimetres below the current ground level, but it was also the first community excavation in Manchester, involving hundreds of individuals, and led to the creation of Britain's first urban heritage park. In the 1980s the main archaeological research within the city was undertaken by the Greater Manchester Archaeological Unit, which was established as a planning and fieldwork county unit and based at the University. In 1994 the field section of the unit was separated to form the University of Manchester Archaeological Unit; a reflection of the rise of commercially funded archaeology in the Britain during the 1990s.

By the end of the 1990s the city centre of Manchester had become one of the four most active archaeological areas within north-west England, at least in terms of commercially funded archaeology (the others being Carlisle, Chester and Ribchester). In 1999 at least 12 separate pieces of developer-funded archaeology took place within the boundaries of

1 The Deansgate Dig, 1972. Run by the University of Manchester Archaeology Department, this was the first public participation excavation within the city. It also demonstrated the survival of substantial Roman archaeology in the Castlefield area of the city and paved the way for the late twentieth-century era of research on Roman Manchester

the city centre, in 2002 this had risen to 21, and in 2007 this had risen again to more than 30 pieces of work, ranging from landscape studies to building surveys and excavations. Whilst the level of developer-funded work reflects the national economic boom of this period, it also is in part a result of the regeneration of the historic city centre after the IRA bomb of 1996. Archaeological units from around the country now regularly undertake commercial rescue work within the city. Yet Manchester's local inhabitants have also expanded their archaeological experience and involvement through community projects such as Dig Moston and Dig Manchester.

Despite all this work there is no definitive modern overview of the whole of Manchester's archaeology and history; a task perhaps too great for any one individual to attempt. The major modern historical work is Alan Kidd's eighteenth-, nineteenth- and twentieth-century social history study, originally published in 1993. Claire Hartwell's 2001 Pevsner guide to the city centre covers comprehensively the surviving built heritage, whilst Stuart Hytlon's historical study of the city published in 2003 deals mainly with the nineteenth and twentieth centuries. The most recent studies on the surviving industrial archaeology remains of Manchester include the Association for Industrial Archaeology's guide to Greater Manchester, published in 2000, which has a separate Manchester section listing 62 of the most important industrial sites standing within the city. Others are English Heritage's guide to the warehouses of Manchester published in 2002 and an overview of the archaeology of Manchester as an industrial city also published in 2002 as the *Heritage Atlas No 4*. Most of the archaeological work undertaken since 2001 thus remains unpublished.

THE SCOPE OF THE CURRENT STUDY

The current study focuses on the modern city and its boundaries as they were in the late twentieth century (2). The growth of nineteenth- and twentieth-century local government has created an administrative Manchester that is long and thin – no more that 10km wide from west to east and 30km long from north to south. Within these boundaries are 34 distinct districts, from Blackley to Wythenshawe and Burnage to Whalley Range, that at the beginning of the twenty-first century were home to around 422,000 people. These boundaries cut across two major river valleys, the Mersey and the Medlock, and follow in the north-west a third, that of the River Irwell. Apart from the hills around Heaton Park and Higher Blackley at the northern end of the city, which are 100m above sea level, the landscape of most of Manchester gently undulates and is no more than 30m to 40m above sea level. Much of this landscape is dominated by clay subsoils, but there are also large areas of glacially deposited sands, gravels and even exposed coal seams in the river valleys of the Medlock and its tributaries.

Since 2001 there has been an upsurge in the amount of archaeological work done within the city and for the first time archaeologists are in a position to recover and record the physical remains of Manchester on a large scale. The emphasis of the current book reflects this new period of investigation. Thus, the book is arranged in chronological

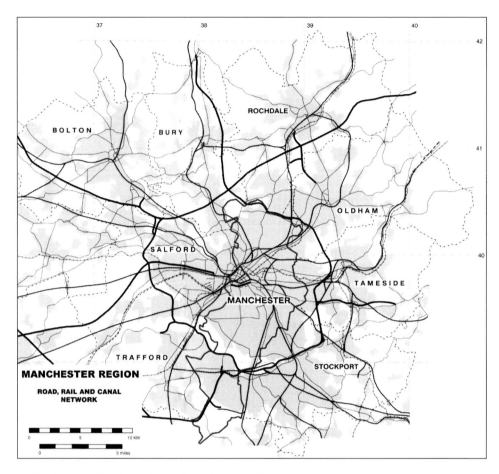

2 Manchester and its city region in the early twenty-first century

order, with two initial chapters on the city's prehistoric and Roman past. Whilst much new material has been uncovered relating to Manchester's earliest inhabitants and to its foundation by the Romans, the bulk of the recent archaeological work has been on the archaeology of the industrial city and this is the focus of the following three chapters of the book. The threat of continued redevelopment to the city's archaeology and the need to retain and preserve for future generations Manchester's legacy as the world's first industrial city are the subjects of the final chapter.

Manchester's influence was and still is felt far beyond its city boundaries. Not only does it affect a hinterland that has been justly called the City Region, but its influence can be seen across the world; through the survival of 'Manchester Goods' in Australia (that is the sale of cotton textiles) and in the dozens of industrial towns and cities named Manchester that can still be found around the globe. The archaeological investigation of the remains of the world's first industrial city is therefore also of importance beyond Manchester itself. This book attempts to summarise for the first time this new work, bringing this hidden history to a wider audience.

CHAPTER 2

THE FIRST MANCUNIANS: PREHISTORIC AND ROMAN MANCHESTER

INTRODUCTION

Manchester is best known for its role in the Industrial Revolution and for its extensive industrial archaeological remains. However, the earliest inhabitants of the city were prehistoric communities. Indeed, the shape of the modern city forms a section across the Rivers Irwell and Mersey – two of the major river valleys in the North West – which would have attracted these early communities.

THE PREHISTORIC OCCUPATION OF CENTRAL MANCHESTER

Prehistoric discoveries from the modern city centre area have been few and take the form of isolated finds of stone tools (3). There are very few remains of the hunter-gathers of the Mesolithic period (first post-Ice Age occupants of these islands, c.8000 to c.4000 BC) within the city, though there are hundreds of small camp sites a few miles north and east of Manchester in the Pennine uplands. Despite the increase in the number of later prehistoric finds from the city region, particularly late Neolithic and Early Bronze Age artefacts and burials sites of the first farmers of north-west England, this growth in activity is not reflected within the centre of Manchester.

At Castlefield, where the Roman fort lies, slight evidence of prehistoric activity came from a recent excavation on the Roman vicus site at 73-83 Liverpool Road. Two Mesolithic flints, one a Neolithic/Bronze Age waste flake and the other a fragment of late Bronze Age/Iron Age pottery, were recovered. Yet all of these artefacts came from redeposited contexts, either Roman or nineteenth century. A nearly complete handmade pottery vessel of Iron Age character came from a second century AD Roman context during the excavation of the Roman fort ditches at the Northgate (Walker 1986).

From the Hanging Ditch have come a bronze dagger, c.5.5in long, and a fragment of a bronze axe. In 1906 Charles Roeder reported to the Lancashire and Cheshire Antiquarian Society that these Bronze Age finds had been discovered in 1880 'during the excavations at the north-east corner of Hanging Bridge, in the old bed of the ditch and under the foundations of the premises now occupied by Mr Ridley' (Roeder 1906, 179). Henry

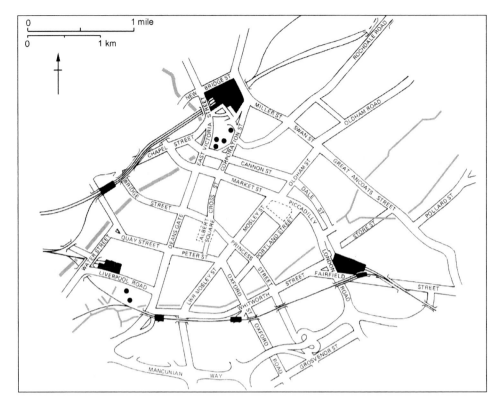

3 The distribution of prehistoric finds within the early twenty-first-century city centre

Ridley was a watchmaker who carried out his business at Hanging Bridge Chambers. In the general locality of Hanging Bridge and Hanging Ditch a flint flake, possibly of prehistoric date, was found by Roeder on the southern side of the cathedral churchyard. A perforated stone hammer dating from the Bronze Age was uncovered in 1870 further to the east, during the digging of foundations at the junction of Corporation Street and Todd Street (Roeder 1899, 205). A flint scraper, probably of Late Neolithic or Early Bronze Age date, was found during excavations carried out by the Greater Manchester Archaeological Unit in 1980-81 on the site of a car park on Long Millgate, but from the published site report this was evidently not found in its original context (Morris 1983, 66).

All these excavated prehistoric finds in central Manchester appear to have come from residual contexts and no prehistoric features have yet been found. In part this is probably because of the rapid expansion of the city from the mid eighteenth century onwards. The scant evidence that has survived suggests that two topographical locations within the city, both overlooking river confluences, may have encouraged later prehistoric activity. The first was the site of the Roman fort, which was in a strong defensive position on raised ground overlooking the confluence of the Rivers Medlock and Irwell. The second was the site of Manchester's medieval castle and church, on a spur overlooking the confluence of the Irk and Irwell on land cut off by a palaeochannel, now known as Hanging Ditch, which acted as a natural barrier. Whether any physical remains for prehistoric settlement have survived the successive rebuildings of Manchester in the nineteenth and twentieth centuries remains to be seen.

THE PREHISTORIC OCCUPATION OF THE MANCHESTER CITY REGION

Evidence for the prehistoric occupation of the wider city region is more extensive than that to be found within the city centre, although it is by no means common (4). A scatter of Early Neolithic flints is known from the middle reaches of the Bollin and Medlock valleys which cross the southern parts of the city. More numerous are stone axes and hammers of the Late Neolithic and Early Bronze Age found in these same areas, as well as the boulder clay-covered ridges that run east to west between the river valleys. There are antiquarian references to a number of barrow sites at Broughton to the north of the city centre in the middle Irwell valley and on the southern bank of the

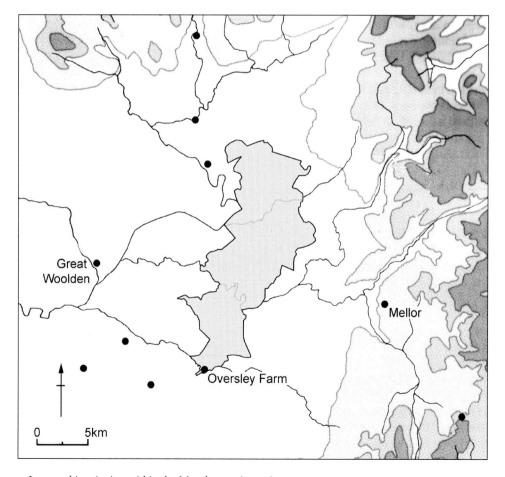

4 Later prehistoric sites within the Manchester city region

Medlock in Gatley. None of these finds and sites has been excavated within modern times.

By far the most important prehistoric site within the boundaries of the twenty-first-century city, indeed one of the most important within the North West, is Oversley Farm (5). This lies on the southern edge of modern Manchester at Ringway on the northern bank of the River Bollin, now beneath the second runway of Manchester airport. Here were found the remains of an Early Neolithic farming community, one of the first such communities to be established within north-west England. These remains comprised what appeared to be a rectangular structure *c.*7m by 10m formed by linear construction trenches and postholes, with a central hearth or cooking pit, dated to 3975-3675 cal BC (Garner 2007, 12-14). This pit or hearth contained a large pottery assemblage of a type known as Grimston Ware, a high percentage of charcoal, fire-cracked stones and traces of barley and crop weed species, implying the cultivation of fields close by. Analysis of lipids within this pottery identified the presence of sheep or goat fat within the fabric of these bowls suggesting that they had been used for cooking (Garner 2007, 20).

The rectangular building was subsequently overlain by a second rectangular structure with hearth deposits dated to 3015-2985 cal BC. A few pottery sherds were associated with it. This demonstrates either a continuity of occupation or a reoccupation and rebuilding on this site of sand and gravel above the River Bollin. This may suggest that this land was regarded as favourable farming land in both periods. The gaps between these two phases raises the

5 Excavations on the site of the Neolithic settlement at Oversley Farm, Runway 2, Manchester Airport (*image courtesy of GMAU*)

question of whether Oversley Farm was a permanent settlement or a seasonal base with religious or ritual significance, as has been suggested at other Neolithic domestic sites.

Bronze Age activity on this site was represented by four-post structures and a 'hollow way', as well as at least two circular buildings associated with pits filled with midden deposits from the periods 2135 to 1660 cal BC and 1000 to 560 BC (Garner 2007). Up to 2000 sherds of Bronze Age pottery were recovered, much of it from the Early Bronze Age, including beakers, cordoned and collared urns, incense/pygmy cups and food vessels. A small amount of Later Bronze Age pottery was represented in the assemblage. A large quantity of lithic artefacts was recovered from Mesolithic and Bronze Age contexts including scrapers and a barbed and tanged arrowhead.

Oversley Farm appears to have continued in, perhaps sporadic, use as an agricultural settlement throughout the Middle and Late Bronze Age, though the small number of features (mostly pits) and the ephemeral structural evidence might suggest less intensive occupation.

Just beyond Manchester's city boundaries lie two Iron Age sites which have been the subject of recent excavation programmes and demonstrate that the Manchester area was permanently settled and exploited by farmers from early in the first millennium BC. Mellor lies 13km south-east of the city centre (6). It is a large upland enclosure of regional importance that nestles in the Pennine foothills. The settlement covers at least six hectares and enclosed several hut circles established in the sixth or early fifth century BC and occupied down to the late Iron Age (Nevell & Redhead 2005). Some 13km south-west

6 The outer ditch of the Iron Age Mellor hillfort, near Marple Bridge, Stockport

7 The late prehistoric and Romano-British promontory settlement at Great Woolden Hall, Salford (*image courtesy of Prof. N.J. Higham*)

of central Manchester lies Great Woolden Hall within the Glazebrook valley on the edge of the lowland bog known as Chat Moss (Nevell 1999) (7). This was a smaller double-ditched enclosure covering a hectare. It contained at least two hut circles and appears to have been a small family farmstead founded in the first century BC and occupied until the middle of the Roman period.

A SETTLED PREHISTORIC LANDSCAPE

The outskirts of modern Manchester contains evidence of human activity from soon after the end of the last Ice Age right through to the Iron Age, when farmers occupied the valleys of the Mersey Basin on the eve of the Roman conquest. We might be able to see only glimpses of the lives of these earliest Mancunians, but we can say that when the Roman legions marched into the Manchester area they were conquering a landscape that had been exploited for thousands of years by hunter-gathers and permanently settled by small-scale farming communities for many hundreds of years.

THE ROMANS AND THE FOUNDING OF THE FIRST MANCHESTER

Towards the eastern end of Liverpool Road, in the Castlefield area of Manchester city centre, can be found a small archaeological park containing the exposed foundations of several buildings, two ditches and a large stone gateway (*8*). These are the main visible remains of the first Manchester – the fort and town, or vicus, established by the Roman legions in the AD 70s and occupied thereafter by Roman soldiers for more than 300 years. The gateway is a reconstruction of how the northern entrance to the fort would have appeared around AD 200. Two ditches were first dug by Roman soldiers and re-exposed in 1980 by archaeologists who were on the site for the first time in nearly 1500 years. It is thus possible to stand on the place where Manchester began.

Mancunians have known for many generations that their city was founded by the Romans. Historical interest in the Roman fort of Manchester can be traced to around 1540 when it was mentioned in an account of the town given by John Leland, antiquary to Henry VIII. Yet interest in Roman Manchester did not seriously begin until two centuries later, when the building of the Bridgewater Canal in Castlefield during the 1760s unearthed a significant quantity of Roman remains, including walls, pottery and funerary urns, which prompted the Reverend Whitaker to write the first detailed, if occasionally fanciful, account of Roman Manchester. Subsequent industrial development in the nineteenth century produced other finds. Their location was often poorly recorded, although a useful plan was compiled by John Corbett in 1850 showing the position of surviving sections of the Roman fort wall visible at that date (Jones & Grealey 1974, 13-19). The modern archaeological study of the fort effectively began at the end of the nineteenth century when Charles Roeder recorded in section and in plan, features revealed during building works for a large metal viaduct servicing the new Great Northern Railway Warehouse, and throughout the twentieth century a succession of excavations, some for research and others ahead of redevelopment work, gradually revealed the extent, character and importance of Roman Manchester.

8 The reconstructed Roman gateway on Liverpool Road, Manchester city centre, stands on the site of the fort and is a reminder of the city's Roman origins

UNDERSTANDING THE ROMAN FORT: TWENTIETH–CENTURY INVESTIGATIONS

The first large-scale excavation of Roman Manchester was carried out in 1906-07 by F.A. Bruton in the north-western corner of the fort, on a site bounded by Duke Street and Duke Place (Jones & Grealey 1974, 18) (9). This identified the line of the western stone wall of the fort as well as some internal features. In 1975 Professor Barri Jones of the University of Manchester excavated a site off Duke Place just to the north of Bruton's

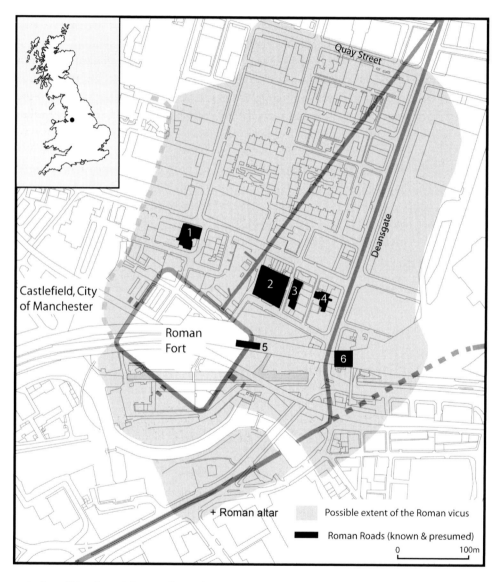

9 A plan of Manchester's Roman fort and vicus showing the sites excavated since 2001. Key to excavations: (1) Liverpool Road; (2) & (3) Barton Street; (4) 340 Deansgate; (5) Castlefield Quay; (6) Beetham Tower (*after Gregory 2007a*)

excavation and found evidence that the fort had been extended on this western side. There was evidence found for an internal building, which from its long narrow plan with frequent cross-walls was identified as either a barrack block or a granary (Walker 1986, 13-20). This building had originally been built when the fort was expanded on the west in the years AD 160-200 and had been rebuilt when the fort was reconstructed in stone in the early third century AD. Further work by the University of Manchester in 2003 revealed the fragmentary remains of the north-western corner of the fort, including part of the sandstone revetment to the rampart and a stone-lined drain possibly servicing the base of a corner tower, all of which dated from the early third century. These features overlay an intervallum road and a sequence of ditches, the earliest of which were two ditches with ankle-breakers cut into the natural stone.

Small-scale excavations were carried out across the northern defences of the fort in the early twentieth century by Phelps (1912), in the 1950s by Petch (1950-1, 1956) and in the years 1965-7 by J.H. Williams (Jones & Grealey 1974, 23-7). These excavations were located in the area between Beaufort Street, Duke Street and Collier Street, and helped to establish the line of the northern wall of the Roman fort as well as providing information on its ditches and location of the northern gateway. The most extensive excavation across the northern fort defences was carried out in the late 1970s and early 1980s on a site at the corner of Beaufort Street and Collier Street. This work was begun by Professor Jones and led to the creation of the Greater Manchester Archaeological Unit, which continued and completed the excavation and undertook its final publication (Walker 1986, 21-60). The excavation straddled the northern defences, encompassing the intervallum road, the rampart, fort wall and northern gateway, the ditches, and beyond these a small area of the external settlement. The results still provide the fullest body of information so far available for the development of the fort. This work led to the establishment of an archaeological park and the reconstruction of the northern fort gateway.

The eastern defences contain the last upstanding section of the fort. This is a short stretch of stone walling, which is now a Scheduled Ancient Monument, and is a survival from a somewhat longer fragment of the eastern wall of the fort recorded by the Ordnance Survey in 1849 (Walker 1986, 3). A.J.P. Taylor rather unkindly called it 'the least interesting Roman remains in Britain' (Jones 1984, 25). At the time he was writing, in the mid twentieth century, there was nothing else to see of Roman Manchester as the fort site was occupied entirely by industrial period warehouses, viaducts and workers' housing. As a result, prior to the early twenty-first century, investigation of the eastern defences of the fort had been very limited. The only significant work in the twentieth century was in 1907 when Bruton dug a trial trench along the eastern side of the standing fragment of the east wall. This showed that the footings of the wall lay on gravels, but it was nearly 100 years before this could be confirmed by further trial trenching in 2005. This early twenty-first century work also showed that the eastern defences had two ditches and revealed the early first century AD turf rampart behind which was the intervallum road (Gregory 2007a).

The least investigated, and therefore least understood, section of the Roman fort defences is the line of the southern wall. Parts of this were reputedly standing when the

Ordnance Survey recorded the line in 1849, incorporated within a row of cottages behind Castle Street. Corbett records that these cottages were demolished in 1850 (Walker 1986, 1–4). In 1998 UMAU undertook an excavation of the floor in the Castlefield Ironworks building and the adjacent car park, prior to conversion into offices. No intact Roman deposits survived and though a sandstone wall was revealed on the correct alignment to be the southern wall of the fort, it was found to overlay a Victorian excavation trench. Similarly at Gail House (the Castlefield Iron Works straddle the line of this wall line) and the Dukes 92 restaurant (on the wall line by the Rochdale Canal) excavations by GMAU in the 1980s found no evidence of intact Roman deposits, though disturbed Roman material was located. Thus it appears that the southern half of the fort had effectively been removed by sand and gravel extraction, and antiquarian excavations during the nineteenth century.

Work on exploring the interior of the Roman fort at Manchester has been equally piecemeal. As we have seen, early antiquarian interest in Roman Manchester was focused upon locating the fort defences and little of the internal plan of the fort was exposed prior to the 1980s.

The disturbance of ground levels in the eighteenth and nineteenth centuries appears to have largely removed Roman deposits in the southern half of the fort. In the 1820s large quantities of gravel were quarried from the fort area and carried by barge along the Bridgewater Canal, together with a number of Roman finds, which were taken to Worsley Old Hall (Jones & Grealey 1974, 15–7). A watching brief, undertaken in 2000 on works carried out below some of the railway arches in the vicinity of Collier Street that cross the site, revealed natural soft red sandstone at a depth of 2m and above this only redeposited material containing nineteenth-century finds.

The northern half of the Roman fort's interior was investigated sporadically during the twentieth century. Bruton was able to sink four trial trenches in a timber yard inside the eastern defences behind Collier Street in or just prior to 1907. These trenches failed to find any intact Roman deposits. The first substantial remains were located by Atkinson in Ivy Street in 1951 and proved to be the foundations of a barrack block (Petch 1950-1, 176–7).

During the 1980s GMAU excavated three areas within the north-western quarter of the fort. At Duke Place, behind the northern part of the western defences, were found remains of a stone building. A second area, at the corner of Beaufort Street and Duke Street, was excavated on the site of the Onward Workshops in 1989. Much of this latter area was heavily disturbed, but cut into the natural gravel were eight pits of Roman date. These pits were c.2m wide by c.0.75m deep and contained repeated sequences of clay lining, charcoal and a gravel layer. One pit was deeper, lined only with clay and contained the highest quantity of Roman finds. Full analysis of these pits has not been undertaken, but the date of the pottery would place them within the late first century and early second century AD, at which period they would have been situated just to the rear of the western rampart. As well as these pits, the excavation located residual features including beam slots and gullies in a narrow strip on the eastern side. From 1987 to 1989 GMAU excavated a series of trenches in Soloman's Arches, below the late nineteenth-century railway viaducts on the southern side of Beaufort Street. A large number of Roman features were excavated, including a section of the northern gateway road next to which was a dwarf sandstone wall (three courses high) for a timber building. Construction trenches elsewhere suggested other structures. There were also rubbish and industrial pits, with four phases of activity represented overall. The excavations in 2005 across the eastern defences revealed details of the interior of this side of the fort showing the existence of a road behind the defences (Gregory 2007a).

Thus, a century of excavation work has helped to establish the form and character of the Roman military presence at Manchester, which can now be seen to be an auxiliary fort established in the late first century. This first fort was a square structure built in timber and turf, 1.2ha in area. In the late second century this was completely rebuilt as a 2ha rectangular timber fort. At the beginning of the third century AD it was rebuilt again, this time in stone (Walker 1986, 141-2).

Whilst the sequence of fort development appears clear after more than 100 years of investigation, establishing which Roman garrisons manned the fort is not. Only five inscriptions record garrisons at Manchester and three of them have been lost. The missing inscriptions all recorded the Cohors I Frisisavonum, an auxiliary unit from Roman-occupied Germany. They were building inscriptions set up by centurions involved in the forts reconstruction. Their date is unclear but it seems likely they were put up sometime during the second century, possibly around the same time this unit was stationed at Melandra Castle near Glossop in the early second century, although the matter is unclear.

Another inscription shows the presence of a detachment from Noricum and Raetia (Austria and Hungary). A second auxiliary unit, the Cohors I Baetasiorum from Germany, is known from an inscription of the late second or early third century. Finally, an early third century altar records a detachment of soldiers called the 'Vexillatio Raetorum et Noricum'. Their status is unclear since the inscription is incomplete. It could refer to either detachment of legionaries from the II Italica and III Italica legions that were stationed in these provinces, or to auxiliary troops drawn from these areas.

A third auxiliary unit is probably attested to at Manchester through the presence of its stamps on roofing and heating tiles. Some time during the first half of the second century the Cohors III Bracaraugustanorum, from Bracares in north-western Spain, were manufacturing tiles for the Roman fort at Manchester and Melandra. Since the unit is unknown elsewhere within Britain and all except one tile that is known from Manchester bears their stamp, it seems likely that they were based here.

Only a handful of the Roman units based at Manchester are known in more than 300 years of occupation.

UNDERSTANDING THE CIVILIAN SETTLEMENT OR VICUS

Though the fort was the first site to be built by the Romans within the city, there is more to *Mamucium*, the Roman name for Manchester, than this purely military site, for the Romans also established a civilian settlement or vicus. Most of what we know about this settlement comes from excavation undertaken since the early 1970s, beginning with the landmark Deansgate Dig in 1972. Not only did this excavation recover, for the first time, extensive evidence for the Roman vicus, it was also the first community archaeology dig within the city, with hundreds of Mancunians, young and old, taking part. Furthermore, it was a major milestone in raising awareness nationally about the increasing threat of redevelopment to archaeology within the historic centres of northern cities (Jones 1984, 23-5).

The investigation of Manchester's vicus falls into two periods. The first was from 1972 to 1981. The Deansgate Dig of 1972 was in an area on the southern side of Liverpool Road, centred on the former White Lion Street, which is now laid out as part of the Roman Gardens (Jones & Grealey 1974). In 1977-78 a fragmentary site was excavated; it is commonly referred to in the literature as Tonman Street, although more accurately it comprised an excavated area on either side of the neighbouring but now defunct Eltoft Street (Gregory 2007a; Jones & Reynolds 1978). During the years 1979 to 1981 a small section of vicus was excavated adjacent to the northern gateway as part of the wider project to investigate the fort's defences. There then followed a hiatus of 20 years, until 2001, when the second era of investigation began. In that year the University of Manchester excavated on a site between Liverpool Road and Rice Street, located c.80m west of the 1972 Deansgate Dig excavation and the northern gateway. An area of roughly the same size was excavated on the eastern side of the northern gateway, immediately east of White Lion Street around Barton Street during 2003-04, whilst in 2004 a small area was examined on the eastern side of Deansgate close to its junction with Liverpool Road, on the site of Beetham Tower. In 2004 and 2005, two small areas fronting both the western and eastern sides of Deansgate were excavated, whilst in 2008 an extensive area around the junction of Chester Road and Great Jackson Street, south of the River Medlock, was investigated. These investigations revealed an organised, industrious, civilian settlement, which was considerably larger than the fort, although its lifespan was much shorter.

The investigations of the 1970s and early twenty-first century, when combined with material found in the eighteenth and nineteenth centuries, have revealed buildings and roads covering a wide area to the north-west, north, north-east and south-east of the fort. The western extremity of the settlement appears to have lain at the western end of Rice Street, the northern boundary around Camp Street, the north-eastern edge in the vicinity of Albion Street (Walker 1986) and the south-eastern edge in the area of Great Jackson Street (Gregory 2007a). This suggests that the vicus occupied the whole of the hill of *Mamucium* on the northern bank of the River Medlock, including the area of the river crossing, and also extended to the southern bank of the Medlock opposite the south-eastern corner of the fort.

This area was covered in buildings, property divisions and roads. Excavations at White Lion Street and Tonman Street both found extensive evidence for buildings, representing several successive phases beginning in the late first or early second century and continuing into the late second or early third century (*10*). At White Lion Street the remains of 13 buildings were identified and at Tonman Street the remains of 15. Further evidence of buildings within the vicus was uncovered close to the northern gate (Walker 1986, 43 &

10 A piece of amphora (storage jar) with the letters ROTAS OPERA inscribed on them from the late second- or early third-century civilian activity around Tonman Street. This has been interpreted as part of a larger inscription which was a word puzzle. When the letters are rearranged they read PATER NOSTER, the first two words in Latin of the Lord's Prayer, suggesting Christian activity at Manchester during this period

46) at an excavation on Worsley Street that went as far north as St John's Street (Jones & Reynolds 1978, 5).

The evidence of these buildings principally consisted of postholes and beam slots, indicating timber-framed construction. In a few cases stone footings were found, possibly for dwarf walls supporting timber-framing (Jones & Reynolds 1978, 14; Walker 1986, 43). The buildings were typically of rectangular form, some having recognisable internal divisions, others being of a single room. The variations also included the addition of a veranda, a building type comprising a shed open along one side and a U-shaped complex around a central yard.

A number of the buildings had a demonstrable industrial purpose, in that they contained hearths for metal working. Close to the northern gateway one particularly small building has been interpreted as a possible shop (Walker 1986, 43 & 46). The earliest building uncovered at the White Lion Street excavation has been identified from its associated finds as a hostelry serving the soldiers and was located in a prime position close to the fort. Other buildings uncovered within the vicus have been construed as having a domestic function (Walker 1986, 131-2).

The majority of buildings at White Lion Street and Tonman Street were sited immediately alongside the northern gateway road. An exception is a building that was sited some 10m from that road. The existence of buildings set back from the road is indicated by the results of an excavation carried out in 1979-81 on a site at Worsley Street, on the opposite side of Collier Street to the While Lion Street excavation. This

11 Excavations on the site of civilian settlement at Barton Street in 2004 produced evidence for extensive Roman activity, including a temple under excavation in this picture

investigation revealed the presence of beam slots and postholes of at least two phases of buildings within an excavated area which lay *c.*10-30m east of the north gate road (Gregory 2007).

The Liverpool Road excavation carried out in 2001 provided the best evidence for the north-western fringe of the vicus (Connelly 2002, 302). The excavation found plot divisions, evidence of small-scale agricultural work, possible evidence of leather preparation and a single building. The site lies *c.*100m west of the northern gateway road and the nature and level of activity found here suggests that it lay on the periphery of the vicus. This was supported by two evaluations in the same area – one adjacent and immediately to the east of the 2001 excavation called the ATS site, which located truncated remains of a Roman ditch, and another 150m west at Woollam Place which found an intact eighteenth-century ground surface with no Roman deposits beneath.

Most of the early twenty-first-century excavations have concentrated on the north-eastern part of the vicus around the junction of Liverpool Road with Deansgate, where redevelopment has been at its greatest in Castlefield.

Barton Street produced the most extensive evidence for property divisions and buildings since the Tonman Street excavations, with four main periods covering at least 10 phases of activity (*11*). In the early to mid second century a series of successive timber buildings were built across the site and these functioned as both domestic structures and workshops. There was a series of pits that may have been associated with industrial processing in this part of the vicus. In the mid to late second century a two-phased building was constructed in the northern half of the site, which was later rebuilt in both timber and stone with what appears to have been a small portico along its western gable. This plan form (*12*), coupled with the building's association with a number of unusual small finds, including what appears to have been a lead figurine (*13*), a zoomorphic mount (*14*) and an urned cremation burial, strongly implies that this was some form of temple structure (Gregory 2007a). Few such religious buildings have been excavated within the civilian settlements attached to northern forts. It is unclear which deity was being venerated at the Manchester temple. The temple structure, along with much of this part of the vicus, was abandoned during the third century.

Excavations immediately to the east of Barton Street, at No. 340 Deansgate, during early 2005, produced a large amount of evidence for such a small site (an L-shaped area roughly 12m by 10m). This included the remains of property boundaries and two associated buildings built during the early second century.

This settlement activity was mirrored on the opposite side of Deansgate at the Beetham Tower site, where in 2004 previously unknown evidence for the vicus in this area was

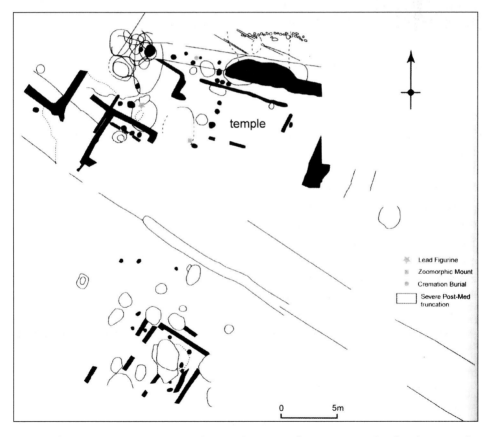

12 Plan of the Barton Street excavations showing the Roman features excavated within the vicus (*after Gregory 2007a*)

13 The lead figurine found close to the temple site

14 The zoomorphic bronze mount found close to the temple site

15 Excavations on the eastern side of Deansgate, ahead of the building of the present Beetham Tower revealed Roman settlement activity in this part of Manchester, including the wall foundations visible in this picture

excavated (*15*). This began with evidence for tree clearance, followed by the fragmentary remains of property boundaries and an associated building built during the early second century, and was succeeded firstly by a period of abandonment, then further building activity which ran into the early third century, by which time the only activity was indicated by a pit and Roman soil layer.

At least four roads are known from within the vicus. Both the 1972 White Lion Street and 1977-8 Tonman Street excavations included part of the road leading to the north gate of the fort. At White Lion Street 10 separate gravel road surfaces were identified, dating from the late first century AD to the fourth century. The earliest road surface was 3.5m wide and was demarcated by substantial ditches. By the second century the road had been extended across the eastern ditch, to reach a width of *c*.6.5m (Jones & Grealey 1974, 30-40). In all, the primary road and later surfaces formed a build-up of over 1.5m. At the Tonman Street site, an unpublished section drawing also shows successive build-ups, in this case surviving to a height of *c*.0.7m and with a width of at least 6m. In the late second or third century, the width of the road at Tonman Street in one place was decreased by an encroaching building (Jones & Reynolds 1978, 14).

Three other roads are known within the vicus. One of these was found in the excavation near the northern gateway in 1979-81. It was *c*.3.5m wide and led from the east side of the north gate road in a northward direction. It has been suggested that this road was constructed to bring supplies from the River Irwell to the fort (Walker 1986, 50-1). A second road led from the eastern side of the north gate road, in this case in a north-easterly direction, and was found on the northern edge of the excavated road at White Lion Street (Jones & Grealey 1974, 53). Finally, two lines of large pits running roughly north to south and either side of Deansgate were excavated at 340 Deansgate and on the site of Beetham Tower. These pits were probably dug to extract gravel for road building and almost certainly point to the building of a roadway along the current line of Deansgate which would have led to the river crossing of the Medlock (Gregory 2007a).

Early in 2008 excavations around the junction of Chester Road and Great Jackson Street revealed extensive but fragmentary remains of plot divisions and pits on the

16 The second century AD Roman altar discovered in March 2008 on the southern side of Chester Road near the river crossing of the Medlock

southern side of the River Medlock adjacent to the river crossing. Amongst the finds was an intact Roman altar of the second century AD set up by one Aelius Sextus, only the second named person we know of in Manchester's history (*16*).

One aspect of the civilian settlement has remained largely unexplored: the cemetery, which lay west of the vicus and fort. In the eighteenth century, Whitaker (1773, 59-60) reported two urns had been found in this vicinity and Corbett's map of 1850 notes that Pioneer Quay, which was excavated in 1849, had been part of a Roman cemetery with 'Many Graves and Relics Found'. Apart from urns of 'common red pottery' there was also a cylindrical rock-cut grave. An altar to Mithras was found on the southern bank of the River Medlock opposite the fort in the nineteenth century. However, the lack of extensive rebuilding work along Manchester's riverfront has meant that this area remains poorly understood.

There is fragmentary evidence that shows that part, if not all, of the vicus was at one time defended by a ditch system. The earliest ditch within this system was excavated on the northern side of the vicus at White Lion Street and was found to run at a right angle to the northern gateway road and parallel to the fort defences (Jones & Grealey 1974, 41-5). A continuation of this ditch has been uncovered to the west on the 2001 Liverpool Road site (Connelly 2002, 302). This may have defined a baggage enclosure associated with the first fort during the late first century AD. The enclosure was abandoned after a few years of use and the vicus expanded into this area.

At White Lion Street the line of a second ditch, this time with a palisade, was identified running northwards from that early enclosure, roughly parallel to the northern gateway (Jones & Grealey 1974, 45-7). What appears to be a continuation of the same ditch was uncovered during the late 1970s in a trench on the northern side of Tonman Street, *c.*40m west of the main 1977-78 excavation. The extent and position of this ditch suggests that it defended the western side of the early vicus (Jones & Reynolds 1978, 7).

On the north-eastern side of the settlement at Barton Street the earliest activity included a large ditch, which dated to the late first to early second century, probably forming part of the military annexe linked to the first fort during the late first century (Gregory 2005, 419). Around 50m to the east, a degraded turf and earthen bank from the late first century was excavated in 2005 at 340 Deansgate. Although the function and form of this bank is not entirely clear, it is possible that it formed an outlying defensive system or an enclosure attached to the early military annexe to the west and north that completely enclosed the first fort. This boundary does not appear to have lasted long before it was slighted, possibly as part of road building for a routeway along Deansgate. However, this bank was also succeeded by a V-shaped ditch and an associated palisade trench in the late first or early second century which probably functioned as defensive features defining the eastern boundary of the vicus (Gregory 2007a).

Since this feature was very similar in style to the palisade trench and ditch excavated at White Lion and Byrom Street during the 1970s and was of the same period, we can now see that the vicus was defended by a ditch and palisade trench on its north-western, northern and north-eastern side, attached in the west to the military annexe during the late first and early second centuries.

Considerable evidence has been found within the vicus for industrial activity in the form of hearths or furnaces for metal work, principally iron working. A total of 33 hearths or groups of hearths were excavated at White Lion Street in 1972. Two main types of hearth were represented (Jones & Grealey 1974). The first and more enigmatic type comprised patches of clay up to 1m across, showing signs of heat and perforated by possible stakeholes. The second is of a more common type in Roman Britain, consisting of a small clay-lined chamber dug below ground level and a short narrow flue. While some of these hearths appear to have been used as smelting furnaces, the principal process here is believed to have been the secondary working of iron blooms to forge weapons, tools or other equipment. In some cases, the hearths uncovered at White Lion Street were set within buildings, while others were located to the rear in the open, with the result that hearths were distributed across the entire excavated area.

Since 1972, evidence for metal working has been found in other excavations in the vicus. At Tonman Street, smithing hearths were located inside two buildings (Jones & Reynolds, 1978, 8). Other hearths have been discovered close to the northern gate (Walker 1986, 37) and at the Worsley Street and Barton Street excavations. The known pattern of hearths suggests that their distribution was densest closest to the fort.

Further industrial activity in the vicus is represented by a pottery kiln found at Tonman Street, c.25m east of the north gate road. This kiln comprised a circular stone-lined chamber fronted by a firing area which was largely taken up by a pit for rakings of ash and charcoal (Jones & Reynolds 1978, 9). This is the only Roman pottery kiln yet discovered in Manchester. There was a pit at the Liverpool Road site in 2001 that may have been associated with leather work.

Palaeoenvironmental evidence, such as seeds, pollen and animal bones, is not plentiful from archaeological deposits at the either the fort or vicus at Manchester. At Duke Place, for instance, a small collection of animal bones, including cattle, sheep or goat, pig and horse were excavated from the upper fills of the late first century fort ditch. Rather than being kitchen or table waste, the presence of horse suggested these bones were deposited together following carcass processing or sacrificial rites. In contrast, the excavations at 340 Deansgate produced evidence for charred seeds from a second-century occupation layer and hearth, probably rubbish deposits; they included oats, barley and wheat, which were all commonly used during the Roman occupation (Gregory 2007a). Such material is typical of many Roman settlements and whilst this is the earliest evidence for arable agriculture in Manchester, as well as the earliest evidence for stock rearing or at least processing, it sheds little light on the civilian settlement.

THE RISE AND FALL OF ROMAN MANCHESTER

What does this long history of investigation tell us about the development of the first settlement at Manchester? Piecing together this evidence, four main phases of activity emerge at *Mamucium*.

17 A reconstruction from 1978 of the timber phase of the northern gateway of the Roman fort as it might have looked early in the second century AD (image courtesy of GMAU)

In the first phase, which spanned the late AD 70s to *c*.AD 90, the first fort was established (*17*). This was square in plan, covering *c*.1.2ha, and was built with a turf rampart and timber gateways. This size of fort probably held a 480 man auxiliary infantry unit. On the north, outside the fort defences, evidence for metal working has been found from this period, whilst this first fort appears to have been surrounded by outer defensive ditches to the north-west, north and north-east, which may also have included a ditched annexe capable of holding extra troops or supplies. The foundation of this first fort is believed to have formed part of Agricola's campaigning in AD 79 to secure the territory of the Brigantes, though in view of the Roman military forts established in the mid AD 70s at the forts of Ribchester and Carlisle to the north of Manchester, the precise date could be several years earlier.

In the second phase of Roman Manchester's life, from approximately AD 90 to roughly AD 160, the timber and earth fort was improved, the rampart strengthened and the northern gateway replaced. To the north of the fort, buildings and iron furnaces were constructed in the vicus which now expanded over the annexe ditches to the north-west and north-east, but was probably defended by its own ditch and palisade. This period of occupation ended with demolition of the fort, involving slighting of the rampart, burning of the northern gateway and possibly the abandonment of the northern vicus. The destruction of the fort may have been due to the redeployment of its garrison further to the north, following the decision of the Emperor Antoninus Pius in the AD 140s to occupy southern Scotland.

Roman Manchester reached its peak in the late second century, *c*.AD 160 to *c*.AD 200. During these years the fort was rebuilt with a turf rampart and timber northern gateway, but possibly with barrack blocks that had stone footings. On the fort's western side, the rampart was relocated further to the west, increasing the size of the fort to around 2ha. It was once thought that the fort was expanded to house a mixed force of 480 infantry and 128 cavalry. However, as a result of the GMAU excavation at Duke Street in the 1980s, it appears that the expansion was carried out to accommodate extra granaries, with the fort serving as a supply depot. In the northern vicus industrial buildings were erected in this period, associated with iron working on a large scale; the unfired pottery kiln probably dates from this period. A street plan of four roads had developed by this stage and the vicus, which now extended to the eastern side of Deansgate and south of the crossing of the River Medlock, included domestic buildings and a temple.

The final phase of Roman Manchester was protracted, lasting from around AD 200 to around AD 400. The beginning of this period was marked by the rebuilding of the fort walls and gateways in stone, although the turf rampart remained. However the vicus showed a steady decline, beginning with the abandonment of the industrial buildings. By the middle of the third century it appears to have either shrunk dramatically or disappeared completely. The fate of the vicus in this period is unclear, as within both the fort and vicus late Roman levels appear to have been removed by subsequent activity. However, the available evidence, particularly from coins, is consistent with the fort having remained in use until the end of Roman rule. By the fourth century, a large outer ditch was dug beyond the fort's existing ditch system, cutting through the road to the northern gateway which was presumably no longer in use and probably indicates that the vicus had disappeared completely.

ROMAN SETTLEMENT ELSEWHERE WITHIN THE MANCHESTER CITY REGION

Whilst the Roman fort at Castlefield was the first settlement established by the Romans, it was not the only one within the city region (*18*). Elsewhere, within the centre of Manchester, other Roman finds are known from the general locality of Hanging Bridge and Hanging Ditch, next to the present cathedral. To the east, Roman pottery was recovered from the University of Manchester's excavations in 1997 at Cathedral Gates, while to the west Roman coins dating from AD 306-340 were found in the 1820s during ground works at the Manchester end of Salford Bridge on the River Irwell (Roeder 1899, 180). Roman pottery was found by the antiquarian Roeder in 1899 at Cathedral Street on the site of the present Corn Exchange in what he reports to have been the remains of a stratified layer at a depth of 4ft (1.2m) (Roeder 1899, 180-1). The precise significance of these Roman finds is difficult to assess. It seems likely that the line of the Roman road from the fort at Castlefield to Ribchester lay roughly in this vicinity, and

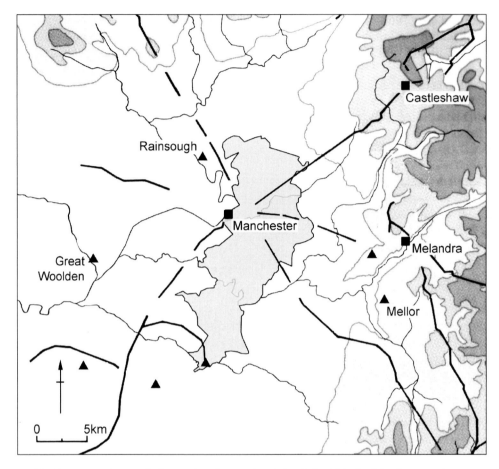

18 The Roman road network, forts and settlement sites (triangles) within the Manchester region

Roeder suggested from the findings at Hanging Bridge that this road may have crossed Hanging Ditch at this point.

Beyond the city other Roman forts are known, for example at Castleshaw, 22km to the north-east of Manchester, which was also garrisoned by the third cohort of Bracaraugustanorum (Walker 1989) and almost certainly at Wigan, 26km to the north-west, where Roman buildings were excavated in the early 1980s and in 2004 a Roman bathhouse was discovered (*19*).

Furthermore, the countryside between the forts and the connecting network of Roman roads was not an empty wilderness. Rather, recent work by archaeologists has begun to show that it was a landscape settled, if sparsely, by small family farming communities. A number of these Romano-British farming communities have been excavated in the last two decades.

At Great Woolden Hall, some 14km to the south-west of the fort, a small ditched Romano-British farmstead of 1.2ha has been excavated on the banks of the Glazebrook, a tributary of the River Mersey. This was first occupied in the first century BC and lasted

19 The Roman forts at Castleshaw in the Pennines to the north-east of Manchester guarded the Roman road from the city to York in the late first century and early second centuries AD (*image courtesy of GMAU*)

into the third century AD (Nevell 1999). The dwellings remained in the late Iron Age tradition, being wooden circular huts, and although Roman pottery from Cheshire, France and Spain was discovered, daily life seems to have been little altered by the Roman Conquest and the building of the fort at nearby Manchester. Seventeen miles to the east lies Mellor, on the fringes of the Pennines, which began as an Iron Age hillfort, but which was also occupied in the Roman period. This too saw little impact from the Roman occupation, other than the import of pottery from elsewhere in the Empire, with circular huts remaining in use well into the Roman period (Nevell & Redhead 2005).

Perhaps the most intriguing of these rural settlement sites is Rainsough, which lies in the Irwell Valley, just 6.5km north of the Manchester Roman fort. Here, a hilltop enclosure of just under a hectare could be found overlooking the Irwell until the early twentieth century, when much of the site was quarried for sand. Two large spreads totalling 761 Roman pottery sherds and some metal work were discovered in the waste heaps from the quarrying on the edges of the settlements in the early 1980s. A small section of banking, strengthened by a double row of posts and running south-east from the enclosure site, was rediscovered and excavated by the Prestwich Archaeology Group, though it produced only one stratified Roman sherd (Nevell 1994, 11–15). This pottery is amongst the most striking material from the Roman period in the Manchester area. Apart from the presence of tegula (roofing tile) which suggests that the settlement had at least one Romanised building, there were eight vessels from mid first century AD, predating AD 85, including Gallo-Belgic wares and terra nigra ware. Rainsough thus appears to have been an important local settlement at the time of the Roman Conquest of north-west England, which makes it all the more frustrating that most of the site has been lost.

CONCLUSION

Roman Manchester was a cosmopolitan settlement with Roman soldiers from Germany, Austria and Hungary, and eastern religions such as Christianity and Mithras. It was also a consumer society with imported wines and fine tablewares from France and olive oil from southern Spain. Such a mixture of peoples and goods traded from afar would not be seen again in Manchester until the creation of the great Victorian metropolis.

CHAPTER 3

MEDIEVAL, TUDOR
AND STUART MANCHESTER

In AD 919 the *Anglo-Saxon Chronicle* recorded that the English King Edward the Elder ordered an army 'to occupy Manchester in Northumbria, and repair and man it' (Savage 1982, 118). This short reference to Manchester was the first time since the Romans left that the city had been mentioned in the historical sources. Between AD 919 and the building of Manchester's second church, St Anne's, in 1709, Manchester slowly developed from a local baronial centre into the most important market town in north-west England. Little of this medieval centre now survives and even less has been investigated archaeologically, but what has been studied throws intriguing light on the roots of the world's first industrial city.

EARLY MEDIEVAL MANCHESTER

Little is known historically or archaeologically of the centuries between the departure of the Romans and the emergence of later medieval Manchester (*20*). Yet this was a crucial period, for it saw the centre of Manchester shift northwards by nearly a mile from the Roman fort to the area around the church of St Mary (the present Cathedral). This new site was a defendable sandstone bluff, defined on two sides by the junction of the Rivers Irwell and Irk.

The abandonment of the Roman fort site is indicated by the absence of any significant archaeology from this area between the end of the Roman occupation and the beginning of the Industrial Revolution (Morris 1983; Walker 1986). The remains of four rectangular pits, ranging in size from 3.2m by 2m to 6.4m by 2.5m and edged by closely spaced stake-holes, interpreted at the time as possible sunken-floored huts of Anglo-Saxon type, and an associated cobbled surface, were found outside the fort's northern gateway and had been dug before that gateway collapsed. However, in the absence of artefacts and radiocarbon testing, both their date and function are uncertain. Later, the stone retaining wall of the fort was robbed and the resulting rubble buried these features, but precisely when this happened is unclear (Walker 1986, 54-8). Both before and after the robbing of the stone the fort and vicus site appears to have been open fields, with the excavations in 2005 at Barton Street and 340 Deansgate producing

20 This tenth- or eleventh-century fragment of Anglo-Saxon sculpture, part of the arm of a wheel-headed cross, was found in the graveyard at Prestwich in the late twentieth century

evidence for an agricultural soil above the Roman levels (Gregory 2007a). During the medieval and post-medieval periods this area remained rural, having become part of Aldport Park, an area of mixed woodland, heath, and pasture.

Elsewhere within Manchester the earliest Saxon evidence in the city is probably the Red Bank urn, which was found in 1850 on one of the rear northern approach roads to Victoria Station in the lower Irk Valley. This is a sixth-century Saxon vessel which may have contained a cremation burial, but its context and precise landscape location have now been lost (Kenyon 1991, 80). A number of later Anglo-Saxon artefacts have also been found. These discoveries include a group of nine *sceattas*, Saxon silver coins of the seventh or eighth centuries from Tonman Street in Castlefield, two early eleventh-century silver coins and a late Saxon brooch and gold ring all from Castlefield. There is a concentration of ninth and tenth century Saxon coins from around the Cathedral area (the junction of the Rivers Irwell and Irk; Morris 1983, 12-15) whilst an inscribed sculpture, the so-called Angel Stone, which might be as late as the early twelfth century, also came from the area of the Cathedral (Morris 1983, 9-12).

The reason for this concentration around the river junction is uncertain, but a clue may lie in the *Anglo-Saxon Chronicle* entry referred to at the start of this chapter. In AD 919 Manchester was on the edge of the Viking kingdom of Northumbria and therefore on the frontier of the Anglo-Saxon kingdom of Mercia. Thus the fact that it was repaired and manned is not surprising and may have been part of a wider policy of defending the frontier of Mercia which ran along the River Mersey (Higham & Hill 2001). This entry tells us that there was a site to be repaired and this supports the finds of Anglo-Saxon material from the city centre. There has been much debate as to where the Manchester of AD 919 lay and the entry could refer to the repair of the Roman fort. Recent excavations on the site of the vicus and eastern defences of the fort indicate a prolonged period of abandonment of the Castlefield area only ended by the expansion of the later industrial city into this area in the mid-eighteenth century. It has been recently argued that the pits in front of the northern gateway may be associated with the refortification of Manchester at this time, rather than being sunken-floored houses (Griffiths 2001), but there remains no fixed date for these features. No evidence of refortification in the early tenth century was found during the recent excavations through the eastern defences in 2005. An alternative suggestion is that the Anglo-Saxon defensive site lay in the area of the present cathedral. This is the area in which the later Anglo-Saxon material was found, indicating that in

AD 919, if not before, Saxon Manchester was focused upon the spur of land that became the centre of the later medieval town.

In the wider city region evidence for the early medieval period is very slight. Settlement and topographical place-names suggest that the transition from Celtic to Saxon culture was gradual once this area had come within the boundaries of the Northumbrian kingdom in the seventh century. The landscape of the Mersey Basin, the river catchment of the Mersey that encompasses an area of approximately 30km radius around the city, contains many place-names with Saxon origins (Chorlton and Withington for instance) and even some with both Celtic and Saxon elements, such as Manchester itself (Higham 2004, 25-7). Names ending in 'ton' (meaning a farmstead) can be found close to the Roman road running from Castlefield northwards towards Ribchester, at Pilkington and Tottington, and suggest that the route remained in use during this period. Both Higham and Kenyon have argued that the unusual density in southern Lancashire of names derived from *'egles'* (the old Welsh for a church) as at Eccles, which lies a few

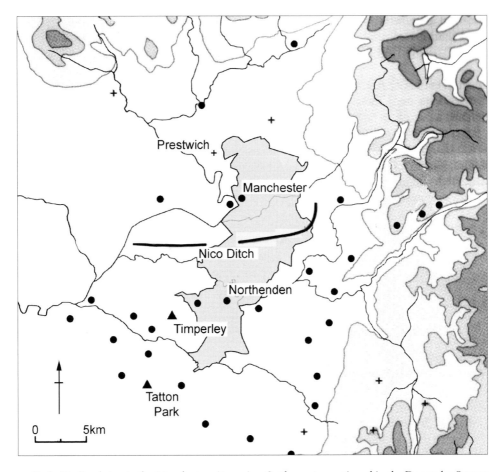

21 Early Medieval sites in the Manchester city region. Settlements mentioned in the Domesday Survey of 1086 are shown as dots. Sites producing Anglo-Saxon sculpture are shown as crosses

22 The Early Medieval earthwork known as Nico Ditch runs across the middle of the twenty-first century city, but the best-preserved section lies on Denton golf course on the eastern edge of Manchester

kilometres to the west of Manchester, may suggest the survival into the Saxon period of a British system of regional churches (Kenyon 1991, 64-68). Late Saxon sculpture in the form of wheel-headed crosses shows that by the Norman Conquest the Saxon church had developed into a network of parish churches, though these probably still covered large areas. This kind of sculptural evidence was found during the nineteenth century in the wider city region from the later medieval parish churches at Bolton, Cheadle, Eccles and Northenden. During the 1990s the arm of a wheel-headed cross with interlaced decoration from the tenth or eleventh centuries was discovered in the graveyard at Prestwich church just north of the city boundary (*20*). How this relates to the later medieval parish of Manchester, which Kenyon has argued was a creation of the tenth or early eleventh centuries, is unclear.

Perhaps the most mysterious feature from this period is Nico Ditch which runs through the southern part of the city and has been interpreted as a late Saxon ditch defining a territorial boundary (Redhead 2004, 18) (*21* & *22*). It ran between Ashton Moss in the east, near Ashton-under-Lyne, and Hough Moss in the west in Chorlton-cum-Hardy. A deed of *c*.AD 1200 from Audenshaw, on the southern edge of Ashton Moss, is probably the earliest reference to this landscape feature and mentions a 'Mickle Ditch', that is a large ditch. For much of its length the ditch only survives as street alignments or administrative boundaries, but there are two well-preserved sections at the Debdale Golf Course in Denton on the eastern edge of the city and in Platt Fields Park, in southern Manchester. Only this latter section has been excavated within Manchester and, like the other sections excavated along its line it failed to produce any dateable finds or any evidence for an associated rampart (Nevell & Walker 1998). This has led to the suggestion that it was dug as a territorial boundary marker rather than as a defensive work.

From the southern edge of the city, on the northern side of the Bollin Valley at Oversley Farm, comes some tantalising evidence for early land use in this period. Four pit alignments were excavated in advance of the construction of the second runway at Manchester Airport. These seem to represent lines of trees, the pits being formed by wind-blown tree loss. The alignments suggest some management of these trees, which possibly defined small fields with dimensions of c.10m-30m by at least 65m (Garner 2007) and were perhaps strip lynchets. Radiocarbon dating of charcoal from pits in three of the alignments produced calibrated dates in the fifth to seventh centuries and tenth to thirteenth centuries. One further site to the north of the city in the Irwell Valley, near to the Whitelow Cairn in Ramsbottom, has produced a late Saxon radiocarbon date. This was a pit filled with bracken ash that might have been used in the fulling process and may represent the first hint of textile manufacture in the city region (Redhead 2004, 18).

LATER MEDIEVAL MANCHESTER

By the time of the Norman Conquest of England in AD 1066, the settlement of Manchester sat on the spur of land between the rivers Irwell and Irk; in the twelfth century here lay both the parish church mentioned in the Domesday Book of 1086 and the little known Manchester castle (23).

The church of St Mary, now Manchester Cathedral, is not only one of the earliest standing structures left in Manchester, it is also one of the finest fifteenth-century collegiate churches in Britain and a reflection of the importance of the town as a regional centre by this date (24). Of the earlier church, little is left to see. Some thirteenth- and fourteenth-century fabric was uncovered during the nineteenth and early twentieth century. The present nave and chancel, each of six bays, are largely mid fifteenth century in date (25). This large-scale rebuilding work is the result of Thomas de la Warre, lord of the manor, who was granted a license by Henry V in 1421 to transform St Mary's into a collegiate church, served by a college of priests (Hartwell 2001, 45-7). The resultant enlarged church was c.47m (155ft) long and had a lofty western tower and elaborately decorated exterior in the late medieval Perpendicular style. This fifteenth-century plan form was obscured by the piecemeal additions between 1470 and 1515 of side chapels on the northern and southern sides of the nave and chancel, giving the church its characteristic large width, and in the early sixteenth century by the building of its fine choir stalls.

One further structure survives from the granting of collegiate church status in 1421 – the domestic premises of the college of priests. This building range lies to the north of the church and is now the home of Chetham's School of Music; it has been called one of 'the best-preserved buildings of their type and date in the country' (Hartwell 2001, 63).

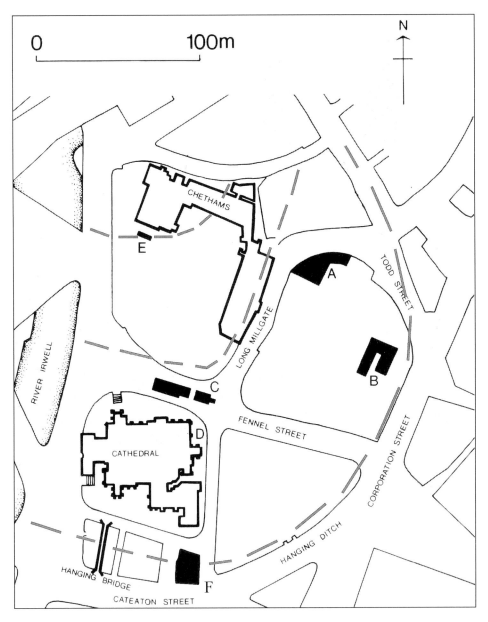

23 The location of the twentieth-century excavations on the site of the core of medieval Manchester – the area around the Cathedral. Key: (A) Hurst Court, 1980; (B) Marsden Court, 1980; (C) Fennel Street, 1974; (D) St Mary's, Manchester Cathedral, 1973; (E) Chetham's College excavations, 1900; (F) Hanging Ditch, 1997. The line of Hanging Ditch and two other ditches possibly to be associated with Manchester castle are shown as dashed lines (*after Morris 1983*)

24 St Mary's, Manchester, is mentioned in the Domesday Survey of 1086, although Manchester itself is not. The current church dates mostly from the fifteenth century, although there are some significant later additions

Bearing in mind there are only three standing structures left from the medieval period in the city centre, their survival must rank as nearly miraculous. The site was given to the new college by Thomas la Warre and appears to have been originally his manor house. However, the red sandstone buildings on the site were erected after 1421 and comprise a gatehouse, ancillary or service rooms, hall, cloister and warden's lodgings. Of these, the open hall is the most complete fifteenth-century building, retaining its original crown-post roof, screens, passage and spere truss.

Manchester Castle is first mentioned in a document from 1184 and disappears from the historic record in 1215. The castle is believed to have stood on the site of the later

25 The fifteenth-century nave and roof at St Mary's, Manchester

manor house of the lords of Manchester, the Grelley family, probably in existence by 1282 (Morris 1983, 36-7) and that was rebuilt as the domestic premises of the college of priests. Two defensive ditches, almost certainly associated with the castle, have been discovered running beneath the present Chetham's School. The innermost of these ditches was first observed around 1900 by Charles Roeder during the digging of a pipe trench to the south of the library of Chetham's School. The ditch was sealed by a surface of boulders and cobbles which Roeder believed to be Roman; the ditch itself he supposed to be Iron Age (Roeder 1899). A short distance to the west, what was almost certainly the same ditch was partially excavated by GMAU in 1980 (Tindall 1983). The excavated section was crossed by a relieving arch for a precinct wall of the collegiate church founded in 1422 and the fill of the ditch produced late medieval pottery. In the light of these findings, the boulder and cobble surface recorded by Roeder was reinterpreted as a medieval culvert over the ditch within the college yard.

A second ditch is believed to have followed the southern and eastern perimeter of Chetham's School along Long Millgate (Hartwell 2001, 7; Morris 1983, 48-9). The existence and line of this ditch was first suggested in the late eighteenth century by the local antiquarian John Whitaker who reported its discovery at two locations in the 1760s; one towards the western end of Fennel Street and the other close to the bank of the Irk. The former Whitaker described as a broad deep ditch three yards in depth below the level of the street; the latter as a rock-cut channel two yards in depth and about three in breadth (Whitaker 1773, 249-50). In the nineteenth century, the antiquarian John Owen observed a third section of this ditch, between Long Millgate and the boundary wall of Chetham's School (Morris 1983, 48 fig. 5b). No dating evidence has been found for this ditch, but it has been suggested that it represents the outer defensive ditch of the Norman castle (Morris 1983, 49).

A third medieval ditch is known from this area of the city and forms the longest and deepest of these features. Unlike the first two ditches, the line of Hanging Ditch, as it is known, can still be traced along the road of the same name and Toad Lane, the latter being later modified, and both roads renamed as Corporation Street and Todd Street respectively. In the late eighteenth century, the local antiquarian John Whitaker suggested that this curving line represented an early defensive ditch, cutting off the spur. Whitaker himself believed the ditch to be Roman in origin, whilst Roeder proposed an Iron Age date (Roeder 1899). Excavation work in 1998 and 1999 confirmed the line of this ditch and showed that it was a large feature roughly 10m wide and more than 5m deep in places (26). Topographically its origin suggests that it was originally a melt-water channel from the end of the last Ice Age, but no finds earlier than the later medieval period have so far been uncovered, suggesting two possible contexts for the deepening and extension of Hanging Ditch (Morris 1983, 47). The first of these is that Hanging Ditch was dug for the late Anglo-Saxon fortified settlement mentioned in the *Anglo-Saxon Chronicle* (Morris 1983, 15). The second suggested origin is that it was dug to surround the later medieval town. At the moment the weight of the archaeological evidence favours this latter, more prosaic, explanation.

The most extensive investigations of Hanging Ditch were the excavations undertaken by the University of Manchester in 1998 and 1999 in the area known as the Cathedral Gates between Cateaton Street and the Cathedral, a site *c.* 50m east of Hanging Bridge. This work was undertaken prior to the erection on this site of the Wellington Inn and Sinclairs public house, dismantled and removed from the Old Shambles. The northern

26 Excavations on the site of Hanging Ditch in 1997 revealed that it had been filled in during the early post-medieval period and property boundaries extended over its line

part of the excavation site had once formed part of the post-medieval churchyard of the parish church, later the cathedral, and included more than 200 burials. The southern part of the site was crossed from east to west by the line of Hanging Ditch, which lay below *c.*3m of cellarage and was revealed in section. The excavation showed that the waterborne deposits within the natural post-glacial channel had been cut to form a broad ditch. The date at which the cut was made is not at present known, but the fill of this ditch contained artefacts and material dating from the fourteenth and fifteenth centuries. These finds included pottery, bone, wood, metal and more than 200 pieces of leather work (both offcuts and leather artefacts such as shoes and a sword scabbard) and amounts to by far the largest assemblage of medieval material from Manchester (*27*). From the excavation it is clear that Hanging Ditch was being infilled by rubbish during the later medieval period, to the extent that by the close of that period the line of the ditch was being reclaimed for building purposes.

Spanning the western end of Hanging Ditch is the third surviving structure from later medieval Manchester – Hanging Bridge (*28*). The earliest known mention of Hanging Bridge occurs in 1343, when it is documented as 'Hengand Bridge' in a property deed

27 Fourteenth- and fifteenth-century finds excavated from Hanging Ditch include leather shoes, off-cuts of leather, animal bones, pottery and a small brass bell

(Morris 1983, 48). No documentary evidence has been found either for when the bridge was first constructed or for the date of any alterations to its fabric. However, a link has often been made with the major building works in the town during the early fifteenth century, such as the rebuilding of the parish church as a much grander edifice served by a college of priests and the construction of a new residence to house that college. The primary function of the bridge can be interpreted as providing an approach to the church from the south, in particular from Deansgate (itself a medieval street) and the town's medieval Marketplace (situated in the angle between Deansgate and Cateaton Street).

Survey work at Hanging Bridge between 2000 and 2002, during ground and building works undertaken for the conversion of adjacent properties into the Cathedral Visitor Centre, revealed further details of this intriguing structure. Most of the known bridge fabric is of a single phase of construction, with the only indication of date being in the use of the four-centred Perpendicular arch, which has suggested the date *c.*1350-1500 (Morris 1983, 48). The northern end of the western face includes a section of more irregular stonework, which has been suggested as being part of an earlier bridge, perhaps with a timber superstructure (Morris 1983, 48). It is possible that this earlier bridge included the lower steps at the base of the south side of the southern arch, which appear to be relatively crude in form. The underside of the arch above these stepped foundations

28 The northern arch of the late medieval Hanging Bridge is still visible next to the present Cathedral. This is one of only three monuments ito survive from medieval Manchester (*Image courtesy of GMAU*)

may include a reused chamfered block. Again no firmer evidence has been found for the date of such an earlier bridge to compliment and refine the documentary evidence for Hanging Bridge being in existence by 1343.

Beyond Hanging Ditch lay the late medieval market town of Manchester. The lord of the manor was granted the right to hold an annual fair at Manchester in 1222 and it can be assumed that a weekly market was also held here by that date. By 1282, the place has become a borough, for a survey of the manor of that date included the rent from roughly 143 burgages (Morris 1983, 38). The extent of this late medieval borough is fairly well known. Fennel Street is attested by name in the Manchester Court Leet records for 1552 and listed as a thoroughfare even earlier. Two burgages mentioned in 1331 were located at the eastern end of the north side of Fennel Street next to the junction with Toad Lane and another, documented in 1473, on the southern side of Fennel Street to the east of the churchyard (Morris 1983, 38-9) (*29*). Fennel Street may have first been laid out when the borough was created or have originated at an earlier date as an access route to the parish church. Extensive archaeological excavations undertaken in 1974 and a watching brief by the University of Manchester in 1999 revealed possible medieval property boundaries, an early road surface and evidence for an eighteenth-century building (Morris 1983, 50-1).

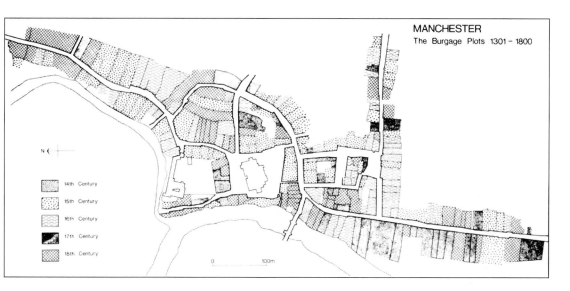

29 A suggested reconstruction of the late medieval burgage, or property, divisions in Manchester, after Morris 1983 (*Image courtesy of GMAU*)

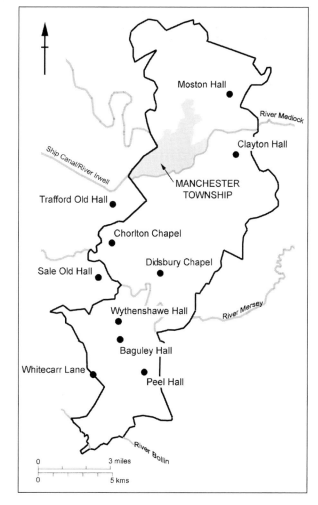

30 Late medieval and early post-medieval sites in and around Manchester

Recorded in the Court Leet records of 1552 was Long Millgate, the manorial mill, and in 1282 a fulling mill on the Irk to which Long Millgate gave access (Morris 1983, 39). Two burgages documented in 1337 are believed to have been located on Long Millgate and others are listed in a rental of 1473, of which 36 have tenants whom can be identified along Hanging Ditch, Withy Grove, Fennel Street, Millgate, The Shambles, Market Street and Deansgate (Morris 1983, 38-9). The earliest known plan of Manchester, dating to around 1650, shows buildings along all these frontages in the core of the medieval borough. Timber-framed buildings of the late medieval or post-medieval period survived along the eastern side of Long Millgate as late as the end of the nineteenth and early twentieth centuries, the best known and most photographed of these being the Sun Inn on Poets' Corner at the corner of Long Millgate facing the entrance into Chetham's School.

Elsewhere around the city there is an equal lack of surviving late medieval remains (*30*). Although the modern city was divided in the fourteenth and fifteenth centuries into a network of small manors, each with its own manor house and farmsteads (some even with their own moat, hunting grounds and corn mills), most of these medieval manors and the evidence for the late medieval economy have long since been built over and lost. There are, though, some notable exceptions – the timber-framed Baguley Hall (*31*), the excavated remains of Moston Hall and Trafford Old Hall, the remains of Peel Hall Moat in Etchells, Wythenshawe, and the recently excavated iron furnaces in Wythenshawe.

Baguley Hall, like that at Chetham's College, is a late medieval hall house with a principal room – the hall – open to the roof. It has been dated to *c*.1325-50 and was built

31 The fourteenth-century timber-framed Baguley Hall, which was later rebuilt in brick

32 Moston Hall, a large late medieval and post-medieval hall and courtyard complex that was excavated between 2003 and 2005

by the de Baguley family. The upper end of the hall was reserved for the family, who may even have sat on a dais, and beyond this were the family's private rooms. The lower end of the hall, where the cross-passage and entrance were located, gave access via two doorways into the service rooms such as buttery, pantry and kitchen. All these elements survive at Baguley and excavations of the hall floor have indicated that the mid fourteenth-century hall succeeded an earlier aisled structure (Hartwell, Hyde & Pevsner 2004, 503-4). One particularly striking feature of its construction was the use of massive planks so that the uprights served as both posts and studs, echoing pre-Norman Conquest Scandinavian building traditions; a similar type of plank or stave construction can still be seen at the mid eleventh-century timber-framed church at Greenstead Church in Essex. However, the tradition seems to have survived in the north-western Midlands and north-western England, for it occurs at the early fourteenth-century timber-framed church of Rushton Spencer in north-western Staffordshire (Nevell & Hradil 2005b) and at the service end of the great hall at Smithills in Bolton. There may have been other examples in this area, now lost.

Between 2003 and 2005, the site of Moston Hall in the northern part of the city was excavated (*32*). These investigations revealed a courtyard complex with late medieval origins, including a timber-framed hall and a stone and timber farmyard range located on a bluff overlooking the Medlock. In 1999 the foundations of Trafford Old Hall were excavated in Stretford, roughly 4km south-west of the current city centre. The hall had been built on a sand and gravel ridge on the southern side of the River Irwell close to the

33 In 2002 a set of three fourteenth-century iron furnaces were found on Whitecarr Lane in Wythenshawe on the boarder with neighbouring Trafford MBC

line of the Roman road from Manchester to Chester. The earliest remains excavated on the site belonged to a timber-framed open hall built on sandstone foundations with an open hearth in the middle of the hall (Nevell 1997). It was demolished in the 1930s.

Sometimes late medieval manor houses had their own moat. These usually date to the thirteenth or fourteenth centuries. In Etchells in Wythenshawe there survives a water-filled moat known as Peel Hall Moat. Although the three-arched stone bridge from the seventeenth century survives, the manor house recorded on the site in the fourteenth century is now gone. The moat at Clayton Hall in eastern Manchester stills retains its hall, although here the earliest fabric is sixteenth century.

In 2002 a set of three iron furnaces, dating to the fourteenth century, were excavated on the line of a new water main on Whitecarr Lane, on the south-western border of the city in Wythenshawe (*33*). Evidence for primary smelting of the iron ore was recovered, along with a scatter of postholes which may have been the remains of temporary open-sided sheds for the iron workers. Why a set of iron furnaces should be located here is unclear, but other lowland iron furnaces are known in the city region from this period, including examples from Gibfield Park near Leigh in Wigan, west of the city, whilst to the north-east along the Pennine fringes in the Castleshaw Valley three further furnaces have been excavated from the thirteenth and fourteenth centuries (Redhead 1996).

At the very least this fragmentary activity demonstrates that the late medieval economy of Manchester was more than just crop growing and hunting, and during the sixteenth and seventeenth centuries another industry would begin its long rise to dominance in the city – textiles.

TUDOR AND STUART MANCHESTER

The earliest known description of Manchester is that by John Leland, Henry VIII's 'King's Antiquary'. Written between 1535 and 1543, he described the place as 'the fairest, best buildid, quickest and populus tounne of al Lancastreshire'. Nearly 50 years later in 1582 William Camden in his great topographical and historical work on England, the *Britannia*, described Manchester as a settlement that

> surpasses the neighbouring towns in elegance, manufacture, market, church and college …
> In the last age it was much more famous for its manufacture of stuffs called Manchester
> Cottons [a coarse woollen fabric]

A fuller description reflecting some of the changes in the previous 100 years can be found in Celia Fiennis' late seventeenth-century book *Through England on a side Saddle in the time of William and Mary*. Thus, in 1688

> Manchester looks exceedingly well at the entrance, very substantiall buildings, the houses
> are not very lofty but mostly of brick and stone, the old houses are timber work, there is a
> very large church all stone and stands high soe that walking round the church yard you see
> the whole town …The Marketplace is large it takes up two streets length when the market
> is kept …
>
> Bradshaw 1987, 8-10

These early descriptions of the town embody much of Manchester's development between 1500 and 1700 (*34*). During this period it emerged as a regionally important trading and textile manufacturing centre, firstly, in the late sixteenth century as the region's pre-eminent woollen cloth town (Roberts 1997, 22-43; Kidd 2002, 15-17) and then in the seventeenth century as the regional centre for both the linen and fustian industries.

The history, economy and social composition of the Elizabethan town is well known thanks to a study published in 1980 by Professor T.S. Willan (Willan 1980). As early as 1551, Manchester cottons – a plain woven woollen cloth characterised by the cottoning or raising of the nap – is mentioned in an Act defining the widths of Lancashire woollen cloth. In 1561-62, five Manchester clothiers are recorded as selling cloth in London (Willan 1980, 56), whilst in 1565 Manchester was chosen as one of five towns in Lancashire for the location of the Queen's aulneger, or officer appointed to examine and approve manufactured cloth (Willan 1979, 175). By the end of the sixteenth century the importance of the town as a centre for marketing textiles was highlighted by the naming of a separate department in London's cloth market as the Manchester Hall (Hartwell 2001, 7). Willan argued that by this date weaving had largely moved out of the town into the countryside whilst cloth finishing remained an urban occupation (Willan 1980, 52-3). This was reflected in the term clothier, frequently found in Manchester wills, inventories and parish registers during the sixteenth and seventeenth centuries. Although elsewhere

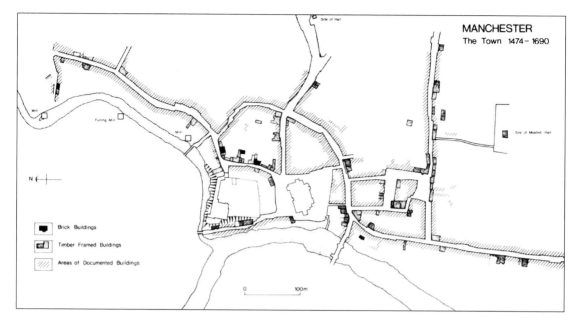

34 A plan of the buildings recorded in Manchester in the period 1474-1690. Most of these were timber-framed properties built in the sixteenth and early seventeenth century from the profits of the woollen trade with London (*after Morris 1983*)

the term covers a variety of functions, in Manchester during this period a clothier was someone who bought cloth from the weavers and often undertook to finish the cloth through bleaching and dyeing, before selling it on.

The growth of the town in the sixteenth century is indicated by the filling of Hanging Ditch in this period. The excavations in 1998 and 1999 indicated that by the mid sixteenth century the line of the ditch had been filled sufficiently to be built upon (*26*). Over the southern side of the ditch, between the Cathedral Gates area and Cateaton Street, were found the sandstone footings of a structure believed to be of sixteenth-century date and apparently representing the rearward expansion, over the ditch, of a property on Cateaton Street. At the same time, a cut within the upper fills of the northern part of the ditch, and a possible culvert above this, suggest successive attempts to maintain a watercourse along the line of Hanging Ditch. This is consistent with the known documentary evidence which shows a continual campaign against the blocking of the watercourse. The ditch is mentioned for the last time in the Court Leet records as an open feature in 1682.

By the end of the sixteenth century a number of wealthy clothiers had emerged within Manchester (*35*). These included William Baguley whose estate was worth £584 on his death in 1573, Thomas Brownsword, whose estate was valued at £1,109 in 1588 and Edward Ellor, worth £323 upon his death in 1596 (Willan 1980, 52-3, 154-5). By far the richest clothiers were the Mosley family. Nicholas Mosley appears to have moved to London in the 1570s from where he and his son Rowland exported Manchester cottons.

He became so successful that whilst he was Lord Mayor of London in 1599-1600 he was knighted. More importantly from a Manchester perspective, Mosley bought the lordship of the manor of Manchester from John Lacy in 1596 for £3,500 (Willan 1980, 9). The previous year his brother Oswald had bought Garrett Hall close to the town and lands in Manchester from Sir Thomas Gerrard, whilst in 1597 Nicholas' son Rowland paid £8,000 for the manors of Withington and Hough. His brother Anthony appears to have managed the Manchester end of the business and on his death in 1607, his estate was worth £2,000, of which £254 was in cloth in his warehouse at home and £224-worth of cloth was at the fullers (Willan 1980, 56-7).

Thus, the Mosleys came to dominate Manchester's mercantile and civil life during the 1590s and whilst there is little to show for their pre-eminent position in the present city centre, the house they built in Chorlton-cum-Hardy around 1596 still stands. This is Hough End Hall and it is one of the earliest and most important all-brick built structures in north-west England (Hartwell, Hyde & Pevsner 2004, 414-6). Its style shows the growing Tudor fashion for more specialised and personal space through an increasing number of rooms, including a ground floor hall and the use of a double-depth plan as opposed to a linear arrangement of rooms. It represents a decisive move away from the timber open hall house that can be seen at Baguley Hall. This structure was built in the

35 The Old Wellington and Sinclair's Public House are the only sixteenth- and seventeenth-century timber-framed buildings left in the centre of Manchester and reflect the wealth of the woollen town during this period

most expensive brick style possible – using Flemish bonded-brick – and was three storeys high, five bays long, including the eastern service wing and western domestic wing, with a large rear staircase. The imposing main northern façade has five stone-coped gables, an array of mullioned windows and a single storey porch. Internally, little remains of the

36 The tower at Didsbury Chapel was rebuilt in 1620 with money donated by Sir Edward and Anne Mosley. The Mosley's had made their fortune in the sixteenth century from the wool trade with London and Sir Edward's father had bought the title of Lord of Manchester.

1590s hall, although the western wing retains two massive inglenook fireplaces (Nevell & Walker 2002, 96).

Nearby in Didsbury church – then a chapel of ease for the Manchester parish – is the tomb of Sir Nicholas Mosley who died in 1612. This is a grand monument that shows Sir Nicholas dressed in the robes of the Lord Mayor of London, along with his two wives and two of his sons (Hartwell, Hyde & Pevsner 2004, 441-2). The short western tower at Didsbury is dated to 1620 (36). An inscription records that it was built with money from his son Sir Edward and Anne Mosley, though whether this was a new tower or a rebuild is unclear (Nevell & Hradil 2005, 76).

Woollen cloth remained a significant feature of the Manchester textile trade throughout the first half of the seventeenth century. For instance, between December 1614 and September 1616 around 28,000 woollen cloths were sealed by the deputy aulnager for Manchester (Willan 1979, 175-83). The traveller Fynes Moryson noted in a visit around 1617 that the town was rich in the trade of woollen cloth, especially those fabrics known as Manchester cottons (Bradshaw 1987, 9-10).

Early in the seventeenth century the linen industry was further developed by the introduction of a mixed cloth called fustian, which had a linen warp and cotton weft. The earliest identified reference to cotton in the Manchester area is usually cited as the will of George Arnould, a Bolton fustian weaver brought before the quarter sessions in Manchester in 1601 (Wadsworth & Mann 1931; Winterbottom 1998, 32). The textile merchants of Manchester rapidly took to this new form of cloth, so that by 1688 Celia Fiennis, who visited the town in that year, could write that 'the market is kept for their linen cloth, cotton tickings, incles [smallwares], which is the manufacture of the town' (Bradshaw 1987, 10). When did this shift from woollen production to linen and fustians take place? A description of the town from 1650 noted that its trade consisted mainly of woollen frizes, fustians and sackcloths, as well as smallwares such as mingled stuffs, caps, inkles, tapes and points (Aikin 1795, 154). This impression is borne out by a recent study of the marriage registers of the parish of Manchester during the 1640s and 1650s by Geoffrey Timmins (1998, 73-4). This analysis suggests that these decades were a crucial period of transition in the Manchester textile industry with the manufacturing leadership in the town passing from the woollen to the linen and fustian trades, and to a new generation of mercantile families.

By the 1620s, three families had emerged as the main fustian dealers and by the mid seventeenth century were the dominant force in the Manchester textile trade (Wadsworth & Mann 1931, 29-36; Willan 1983, 37). These were the Booths, the Chethams and the Wrigleys, the Mosley family having retired from trade to take up their life as lords of the manor of Manchester (Wadsworth & Mann 1931, 30-4). Perhaps the wealthiest of these families was the Chethams.

In his will of 1653, Humphrey Chetham left several thousand pounds as a bequest to found a Blue Coat grammar school and free library in the ruinous buildings of the former college of priests next to the parish church; this conversion took place in the years 1654-58. The original college had been dissolved in 1547 and after that the buildings had lain derelict. Under the terms of his will they were converted into a school and library, both functions the buildings retain in the early twenty-first century. This conversion work involved the addition of a fireplace and stairs in the hall and the conversion of the ground floor apartment above the hall into the audit room where the feoffees (trustees) of Chetham's charity held their regular meetings. The new decorative features in this room included panelling and plaster work which can still be seen (Hartwell 2001, 65). The room above was re-panelled in this period. The most impressive of the 1650s furnishings is the survival of the original chained library with its books and bookcases, the latter built in the years 1655-8 by a local joiner and surveyor called Richard Martinscrofte (Hartwell 2001, 68-9).

Another prominent mid seventeenth-century textile family were the Byroms, who were linen drapers. In 1657 the family rented a town house in the Shambles Market in Manchester, which they then bought in 1666 – the Old Wellington. The building was re-erected and restored on its present site next to the Cathedral, in Hanging Bridge Street, in 1999. Originally, it stood on the southern side of the Shambles Marketplace and was leased to Edward Byrom in 1657. The family retained ownership of the building that became the Old Wellington until the nineteenth century (37). Byrom's will from 1669 indicates that what survives is merely a fragment of a much larger mercantile property that included two warehouses, a brewhouse and a kitchen, probably arranged around a courtyard to the rear, or immediately south of the building, accessed via an alleyway on the western side of the Old Wellington. The current three bay, three-storey domestic building covers roughly 225m². The lower two storeys date from the mid sixteenth century, whilst the third storey was added in the seventeenth century, though its style was no later than 1660, and probably some years before Edward Byrom leased the property in 1657. Such a courtyard arrangement, with its mixture of domestic and commercial textile buildings, appears to have been common in seventeenth-century Manchester, although this is the only one to survive.

37 The northern elevation of the Old Wellington and Sinclair's as it was before being moved in 1990, showing the purchase of the various parts of the property held by the Byrom family, one of the most prominent woollen trading families in seventeenth- and eighteenth-century Manchester

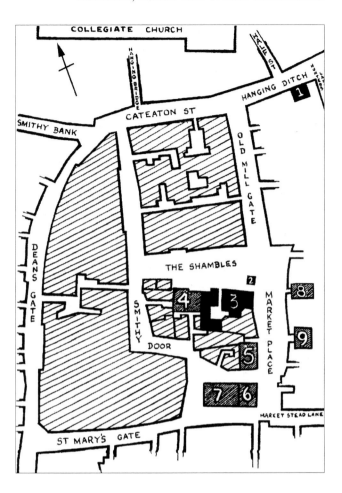

38 A reconstruction of the seventeenth- and eighteenth-century commercial heart of Manchester, the Shambles and Marketplace areas, showing the Byrom family's properties, Nos 1 and 3. Key: (1) Byrom town house; (2) Market Cross; (3) Old Wellington Inn with textile warehouses to the rear around the courtyard; (4) John Shaw's Punch House, now Sinclair's; (5) Court Leet house; (6) The Conduit House, containing Manchester's first piped water supply; (7) the 1729 Exchange; (8) Bull's Head; (9) Angel Inn (*after Nevell 2003, 33*)

Elsewhere within the city centre little remains of this sixteenth- and seventeenth-century textile boom town, with its four marketplaces, sessions house, merchants' houses, warehouses and public fountain (*38*). The 1650 map of Manchester shows a town spread along Deansgate, Long Millgate, Market Street and up Shudehill, where until the late nineteenth century there were many timber-framed buildings predating the mid seventeenth century and thus the product of this early woollen and linen textile boom period (*39*). In 1980-81, excavations on the site of Mardsen Court between Fennel Street and Corporation Street revealed three rubbish pits containing late seventeenth-century pottery to the rear of properties on the northern side of Fennel Street (Morris 1983, 56-7). To the north of this site an area on the southern side of Long Millgate was also excavated in 1980-81 but the only early features in this area, probably from the seventeenth century, were the sandstone foundations for a rectangular-plan timber-framed building and a sandstone-lined well which may have been contemporary (Morris 1983, 57-8).

Excavations in 2007 on the site of the Pump House, at the junction of Left Bank and Bridge Street on the eastern bank of the Irwell, have shown that before this area was built upon in the early to mid eighteenth century it was used as a rubbish dump. This was

39 A nineteenth-century view of Smithy Door, a road at the western end of the Shambles. The tower of Manchester Cathedral can be seen at the end of the lane, whilst the Old Wellington complex is to the right

40 The chapel at Chorlton-cum-Hardy was built in 1512 and is one of several late medieval timber-framed chapels that could be found in the Manchester area

perhaps waste from the properties at the northern end of nearby Deansgate and the finds included an extensive array of seventeenth-century pottery. A similar river-side rubbish dump has been excavated on the western bank of the River Irwell on the edge of the ancient borough of Salford. At several sites along Chapel Street, late medieval, sixteenth- and seventeenth-century property boundaries have been excavated, running eastwards down the river bank to the Irwell and all have produced evidence for successive periods of rubbish dumping on the river's edge.

Outside of the city centre, remains of the sixteenth- and seventeenth-century landscape of the Manchester area survive primarily in the form of the standing and excavated halls (*30*). Although the southern suburb of Northenden was a small village clustered around the ancient medieval parish church of St Wilfrid, little can be seen above ground from before the eighteenth century. Late medieval chapels of ease could be found in the parish of Manchester at Didsbury, Gorton and Stretford, but only Didsbury and Stretford had an associated village during the sixteenth and seventeenth centuries and, as at Northenden, nothing this early now remains above ground at either place. Several timber-built chapels were founded in the sixteenth century, at Chorlton-cum-Hardy in 1512, Denton in 1531, Blackley in 1548 and Newton Heath in 1573 (Hartwell, Hyde & Pevsner 2004, 27), but again these were isolated buildings in a sea of fields and only St Lawrence's in Denton, now in Tameside, retains any substantial timber-framed fabric from this period (Nevell & Hradil 2005b) (*40*).

Beyond these small villages and chapels of ease was a countryside which in the sixteenth and seventeenth centuries was dominated by isolated and dispersed halls and farmsteads. The predominance of the isolated farm in the settlement pattern of the North West can be traced back as far as the thirteenth and fourteenth centuries (Brennand with Chitty & Nevell 2006) through the distribution of more than 100 moated sites and around

41 Wythenshawe Hall in southern Manchester was a timber-framed manor house of the late medieval period which was rebuilt and extended in the mid-sixteenth century by the Tatton family

350 cruck buildings in north-western England. The presence of moated sites in this distribution pattern, concentrated within south-east Lancashire and northern Cheshire, would suggest that some local lords were taking part in the clearing of new woodlands and thus helping to create this dispersed settlement pattern, most notably in the medieval Hundred of Salford around Manchester. The surviving archaeological evidence from the sixteenth and seventeenth centuries indicates that the landscape had become cluttered with such isolated domestic sites. Yet of the hundreds of such sites recorded in this period, very few have survived into the twenty-first century, and those that have tend to be the higher status buildings such as halls, rather than the farmhouses of the local tenantry.

Within the boundary of the wider city, the surviving buildings of the sixteenth and seventeenth centuries are almost exclusively the halls of the local landowners: Barlow Hall, Clayton Hall, Hough Hall in Moston, Slade Hall, and Wythenshawe Hall. Clayton Hall and Wythenshawe Hall have medieval origins, but Clayton is the only one of this group to have been moated (*41*). The moat is now dry, but a seventeenth-century twin-arched stone bridge leads to the platform on which stands two bays of a fifteenth- or sixteenth-century hall house with a late seventeenth-century brick wing. From the twelfth to the early seventeenth century it was the home of the Byrom family and thereafter of the textile merchant Humphrey Chetham. Wythenshawe Hall, the home of the Tatton family from the thirteenth to the early twentieth century, was rebuilt in the mid sixteenth

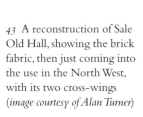

42 Excavations at Sale Old Hall opposite Chorlton-cum-Hardy indicated that this manor house was a completely new build of around 1600

43 A reconstruction of Sale Old Hall, showing the brick fabric, then just coming into the use in the North West, with its two cross-wings (*image courtesy of Alan Turner*)

century; a timber-framed hall range flanked by two cross-wings survives. Barlow Hall, Hough Hall in Moston and Slade Hall in Levenshulme all appear to have been new timber-framed buildings of the mid sixteenth century, each with a hall, a parlour above and cross-wings.

The excavated domestic sites within and around the city of this period are also higher status dwellings. These include the courtyard complex of Moston Hall to the north of the city centre and Denton Hall just across the eastern border of the city, which was a thirteenth-century moated timber hall house that was rebuilt in the early sixteenth century, but which retained its open hall, as did Trafford Old Hall to the south-west. When Sale Old Hall, on the southern side of the River Mersey opposite Chorlton-cum-Hardy, was excavated in 2004, it was found to be a completely new brick hall of the late sixteenth century with a double-depth room plan flanked by two cross-wings, rather like Hough End Hall (*42* & *43*).

'THE FAIREST BEST BUILDID...TOUNNE'

In 1688, Celia Fiennis talked about a town with 'very substantiall buildings, the houses are not very lofty but mostly of brick and stone, the old houses are timber work ...'. Yet all that is left of sixteenth- and seventeenth-century Manchester is the Old Wellington public house and the street pattern; Hanging Bridge, Withy Grove, Long Millgate, Shudehill, Market Street, Deansgate and the Shambles – the roads shown on the *c.*1650 map of the town. In 1709, St Ann's church was founded by Sir Edward Mosley's daughter and heir, Lady Ann Bland, who died in 1734 (Hartwell, Hyde & Pevsner 2004, 442) and in 1720 St Ann's Square, south of The Shambles and east of Deansgate was laid out. The building of this church and its associated square marked the beginning of a new chapter in Manchester's development; its rise to national prominence as a Georgian textile boom town.

CHAPTER 4

THE GEORGIAN BOOM TOWN

Between 1724 and 1726, Daniel Defoe, novelist, political writer and spy, undertook a tour of Britain and amongst the many places he visited was Manchester. His description of the town as 'one of the greatest, if not really the greatest mere village in England' is so well known as to be almost a cliché, but he was not the first visitor, nor the last, to comment upon the town's lack of government and the commercial advantages that flowed from that situation. In 1704 the Bishop of Carlisle, having stayed in Manchester, noted that 'the Town is no Corporation or Borough; but the largest ville in the Queen's dominions' (Bradshaw 1987, 11-2). Joseph Ashton concluded in 1816 that the absence of a corporation or borough to govern the town 'induced strangers to add their stock of property, industry, and talent, to the growing prosperity [raising] the town and trade of Manchester to its present consequence on the national scale' (Bradshaw 1987, 31). It was to be 1838 before Manchester became reinstated as a borough, by which date the town had risen to become one of the six largest towns in Britain and the largest factory town in the country; in other words it became the first industrial city in the world. A sense of the scale of this mercantile booming 'mere village' was given in 1805 by the historian John Briton, who declared that 'Manchester is an immense manufacturing, mercantile and trading town, consisting of a great number of streets, lanes, alleys, and courts, which are crowdedly filled with warehouses, factories and shops' (Bradshaw 1987, 23). Clearly Manchester was viewed increasingly during the eighteenth century as being exceptional for both its lack of government and the size and character of its industry, yet until recently very little was known about the archaeology of this Georgian boom town. Since 2002 a series of major excavations and small-scale evaluations has begun to reveal how dynamic and rapid this expansion was.

MANCHESTER'S POPULATION, 1563 TO 1801

One of the most troublesome questions about the city during this period is whether the population expansion of Manchester was a consequence of the town's rise as a manufacturing centre or the prime mover in its industrial development. An answer to this issue is made harder by a lack of reliable data. The 1838 borough was much bigger

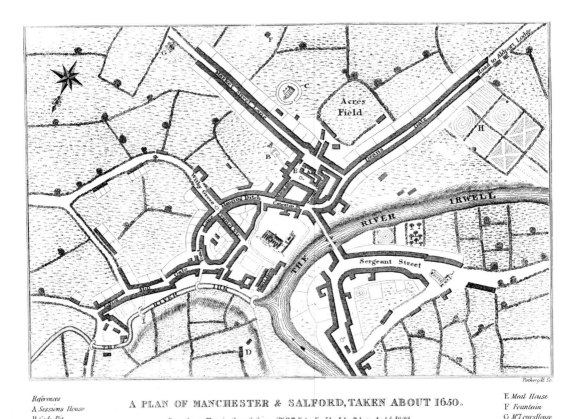

References
A *Sessions House*
B *Cock Pit*
C *Radcliffe Hall*
D *M Knowles House*

A PLAN OF MANCHESTER & SALFORD, TAKEN ABOUT 1650.

Drawn from a Plan in the possession of William Yates Esqr by John Palmer Archt 1822.

E *Meal House*
F *Fountain*
G *M Leversllouse*
H *New Gardens*
I *Tanner Bridge*

44 The earliest map of Manchester dates from around 1650, although only a later copy survives. At this date the city covered little more than the area around the cathedral and Chetham's School

than its medieval counterpart, but accurate population figures for Manchester were not taken until the census of 1801 (Hartwell 2001) (*44*). Nevertheless, there are a number of points during the period 1563-1801 that give an indication of both Manchester's size and rate of expansion (Nevell 2003).

The earliest record of population for the Manchester area in this period comes from 1520 which gives a figure of 7000 for the parish, although this was clearly many times larger than the township (Wadsworth & Mann 1931, 509). Willan suggested that the township had a population of 1800 for the year 1563, based upon the number of households given in the episcopal returns to the Privy Council in that year (Willan 1980, 38-9). The next approximation of Manchester's population can be made in February 1642, when all householders and men of 18 years or over within the township were called upon to sign the Protestation, a political document expressing their willingness to maintain the Anglican Church and to protect the King's person and the freedom, rights and liberties of the subject. This record lists around 1200 names suggesting a population for the township of just over 3000 (Willan 1980, 39; Willan 1983, 36). This figure is lent some support by the Hearth

Tax Returns of 1664, which list 820 households, suggesting a population of around 3690 (Arrowsmith 1985, 100; Phillips & Smith 1994, 7). These figures suggest that Manchester's population roughly doubled in the years 1563 to 1664, well above not only the national average increase of 68 per cent, but also the North West's average of 64 per cent and the Lancashire average of 72 per cent during this period (Phillips & Smith 1994, 6-7). It is worth noting that this growth was not consistent nor uninterrupted, for on three occasions during the period 1563 to 1664, the population was considerably reduced as a result of outbreaks of plague, during the years 1565, 1605 and 1645 (Arrowsmith 1985, 100-101; Willan 1983, 29-40). Was this growth entirely internal? Willan's sixteenth- and early seventeenth-century studies suggest that this was probably not the case. Whilst the evidence for migration into the town is scant, the very fact that Manchester's population rapidly recovered from these three plague outbreaks strongly suggests that the population shortfall was made up by a significant number of migrants from the surrounding countryside. This migration is probably reflected in the Court Leet records that distinguish in this period between natives and foreigners (Willan 1979, 175-83; Willan 1980, 38-9, 80; Willan 1983, 39). The reason for this immigration into the city is not explicitly stated, but Manchester's growing position as a leading market and manufacturing town seem likely causes.

Manchester's growth during the 109 years from 1664 to 1773 was even more startling, with the township growing nearly seven-fold (45). The first indication of Manchester's

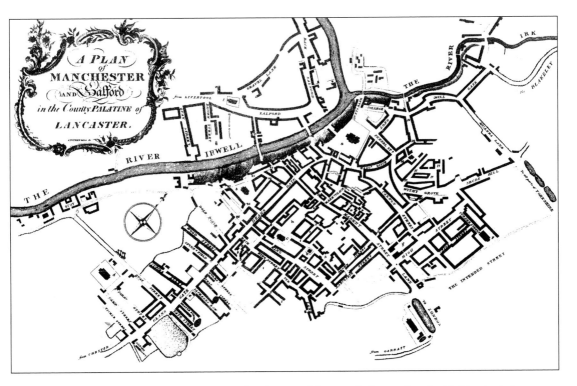

45 The 1773 map of Manchester indicates that the area of the town had more than doubled its physical size since 1650

accelerating growth is given in the Bishop of Chester's returns for 1717 that lists the number of families in the township as 2003, suggesting a population of around 9000, more than double the figure for 1664. Both Daniel Defoe and William Stukeley visited the town around 1724 and passed comment on the number of its inhabitants. Defoe estimated the population of Manchester and Salford at around 50,000, which seems far too high (Arrowsmith 1985, 101), whilst Stukeley's estimate that the Manchester township had roughly 2400 families is closer to that recorded by the Bishop's returns of 1717. The next indicator of Manchester's expanding population comes in 1758, when an enumeration of the population of the township was prompted by a dispute over the manorial corn mill, and suggested that the township, but not the town, contained 17,101 people, a near doubling in the previous 40 years and a slightly faster rate of growth than in the period 1664-1717 (Arrowsmith 1985, 101).

The census of 1773 is usually taken as the most accurate prior to that of 1801. This was organised by a private group led by the antiquarian and local historian John Whitaker. The census indicated that the township of Manchester contained 24,937 people, of whom 23,032 lived within the town itself, indicating that in the preceding 15 years Manchester's population had grown by 35 per cent or just over a third (Arrowsmith 1985, 101). Again this was a further acceleration in the rate of population growth compared to the period 1717-58. This increased rate of growth was eclipsed by the rapid expansion of the final quarter of the eighteenth century. The 1801 census records 70,409 people within the town, a trebling of the town's size in the space of a generation, which was hitherto totally unparalleled in Manchester's history.

The tracing of the growth of Manchester's population is important in this period because it allows us to put the town in its regional and national contexts, with much of the expansion being the result of inward migration from the North West and later from Ireland, Scotland and Wales. In 1500, Manchester was one of the smaller 34 market centres in the region (Morris 1983, 21), but by 1664 it had grown to become the largest town in Lancashire and probably the fourth biggest in the region behind Chester (with a population of around 7800) Macclesfield and Nantwich, both of which had similar population sizes to Manchester's (Phillips & Smith 1994, 7). Whilst population size remains difficult to establish throughout the period, it is clear that by 1720 the two largest urban centres in North West England were Liverpool and Manchester, both with populations around 10,000, according to Gastrell's census of that year (Phillips & Smith 1994, 67) (46). The next largest urban centre in the region was Chester, which in 1728 is thought to have had a population of around 8700.

Nationally, by 1801, Birmingham, Liverpool and Manchester were the largest urban centres outside London, each with populations around 70,000, and there were only two other towns with populations in excess of 50,000 (Bristol and Leeds). In 1801 there were eight towns with populations between 20,000 and 50,000, and 30 with populations between 10,000 and 20,000 (Prince 1973, 458-9). Yet the next largest north-west towns in 1801 were Chester and Stockport, both with populations of around 15,000. The fastest rate of population growth for Manchester in this period occurred in the years after 1773. These coincided with the building of the first textile mill within the city in 1781-82 and

46 When Hanging Ditch was excavated in the late 1990s it was found that the graveyard to the south of St Mary's had been extended over this area in the seventeenth and eighteenth centuries, reflecting Manchester's growing population in this period

a subsequent mill building boom, which meant that by 1801 there were more than 33 mills in Manchester.

Demonstrating a direct link between the arrival of this factory system, with its need for a large-scale local work force, and Manchester's accelerating population growth, is not straightforward. The earliest physical evidence for a big expansion in housing comes not from the 1780s and 1790s, but from the 1750s, 1760s and 1770s, and coincides with the rise of fustian production, in the form of weaving, within the town, the building of Manchester's first wharf, on the River Irwell, and the Bridgewater – the city's, and Britain's, first industrial canal.

THE PROTO–INDUSTRIAL FUSTIAN BOOM TOWN

The eighteenth century marks the emergence of Manchester as a manufacturing and commercial town of regional importance, but within the cotton trade rather than the linen branch of the textile industry, which was in sharp decline within the town after 1700 (Chaloner 1955, 157-8) (*47*). The dominant position of Manchester in the newly developing cotton manufacturing trade of the early eighteenth century is reflected in two ways; firstly in the probate evidence for the period 1700-60. Superficially this evidence reveals that most textile production was rural-based; around three quarters of all linen and cotton manufacturing taking place in the countryside, with woollen production being evenly split between the town and country (Stobart 1998, 7). Closer analysis revealed that silk and smallware manufacture and textile finishing were all largely urban-based and that Manchester dominated this urban textile trade as both a regional and local manufacturing centre (*48*). For instance, half of all the probate records for the finishing trades during this period were Manchester-based. The growing importance of cotton in Manchester's textile trade is reflected in the references to fustians, at this period, in the probate evidence, which rose from zero in 1700 to 30 per cent of all textile occupations listed in the Manchester probate records by the mid eighteenth century (Stobart 1998, 7). Textiles dealers (often though not exclusively referred to a chapmen in these records) were three times more likely to be urban-based and once more Manchester was the regional centre for such dealers (Stobart 1998, 12-13). The putting-out system was by no means universal in this period, Manchester and its chapmen were already central to the trade. Its textile merchants 'not only controlled the supply of raw materials

47 St Anne's church, built during the years 1709-12, was founded by Lady Ann Bland, née Mosley, and reflects the continuing influence of the Mosley family on Manchester's life into the eighteenth century. The current tower was rebuilt in 1777. The building of St Anne's was one of the signs that Manchester was emerging as a regional urban centre

48 Mersey Flats sailing boats unloading at the warehouses below St Mary's, Manchester, around 1734

and the marketing of the finished cloth … but also played an increasingly important part in determining the work-patterns of the individual workers' (Stobart 1998, 13). An example of this can be found in the will of Joseph Jolly, linen draper of Manchester, who died in 1753 leaving £431 17s 3d of goods in his warehouse and a further £548 9s 6d in the weighhouse. His will lists 137 individuals to whom debts were owed or credit was extended, including 13 yarn winders and 42 weavers (Stobart 1998, 14).

Secondly, Manchester's dominant position is reflected in the passing of the Manchester Act in 1736. This prohibited the manufacture of all-cotton cloth in Britain and was designed to protect the woollen industry against competition from the new, cheap, all-cotton materials imported from India and from cotton cloth being made in this country, whose production centre was the Manchester area. Fustians, the manufacture of which was dominated by the Manchester textile merchants, were permitted to be made but were subject to a tax of 3d per yard. The Act was repealed in 1774, largely through the efforts of Richard Arkwright.

The rising prosperity of the Manchester textile merchants and the success of the putting-out system is illustrated by the life of Joseph Byrom, owner of the Old Wellington and Boroughreeve in 1703 (Thompson n.d.), who in the period 1675 to 1733 amassed an immense fortune (37). After an eight-year apprenticeship in textiles he set himself up as a fustian and silk merchant in 1683, trading between Manchester and London. By 1702 his estate was worth £7,000 and this had risen to £12,900 by 1715. He bought the property next door to the Old Wellington from his brother in 1713 for £1,320; this now forms part of Sinclair's. In 1721 his estate was worth £14,400 and his townhouse was situated in the Blue Boar Court, adjacent to the Marketplace – the heart of the textile commercial district in eighteenth-century Manchester. His will of 1733 shows that besides land in Manchester including the Old Wellington, the house in Blue Boar Court and lands to the west of Aldport, he held property in Barton, Deane, Halliwell, Stockport and Urmston, as well as owning the Smithills Hall, one of the great medieval houses of the North West, which he had bought for £4,688 in 1722.

Byrom's son, Edward, remained involved in the textile and mercantile trade of Manchester until his death during the 1770s. In particular, Edward was an important shareholder from 1735 onwards in the Mersey and Irwell Navigation Company, created by an Act of Parliament in 1720 at the instigation of a group of Liverpool and Manchester landowners, and merchants including his father. He became chairman of the company in 1757, leading a committee dominated by Manchester merchants, whom during the 1750s and 1760s included John Bower, Thomas Chadwick, Robert Gartside, John Hardman and Marsden Kenyon (Nevell 2005). Some of his wealth he used to build a number of properties around the town and provided the money to build St John's church off Deansgate in 1769.

Recently, the remains of the industrial premises of another of Manchester's mercantile families were excavated on the northern side of Hardman Street, to the west of Deansgate (49). In the 1740s, Casson and Berry's map of Manchester shows that this area was occupied by a substantial building and its grounds, identified in the key to the map as 'Mr Bower's House'. Miles Bower Sr and Miles Bower Jr appear to have been prominent figures in eighteenth-century Manchester, who derived their wealth from the town's role as a centre of felt hat manufacture. The younger Miles Bower's death in February 1756 was recorded in a contemporary account as follows: 'last night died after a short illness at his house the upper end of Deansgate Mr Miles Bower Junr a very considerable dealer in hats much esteemed by his acquaintance, and makes his death greatly lamented' (Manchester Central Libraries, Owen Ms 23, 299).

Miles Bower Sr seems to have continued to live at the house on Deansgate until his own death in 1780, at the age of 85. In October 1771, the death was recorded of Mrs Bower 'wife of Mr Miles Bower in Deansgate', while in the first Manchester and Salford directory, published in 1772, Miles and John 'Bowers', are listed as hatters in Aldport Lane (Manchester Central Library, Owen Ms 23, 299, 301; Raffald 1773). Between the 1730s and 1750s, the two Bowers served as jurors on Manchester's manorial court, the Court Leet, and on occasion held the office of constable. In 1740, Miles Bower was charged by officers of the court with the public nuisance of dumping a midden on a public thoroughfare; his presentment to the court refers to him as a 'feltmaker', the earliest reference found to date for the family's involvement in the hatting trade (Earwaker 1888).

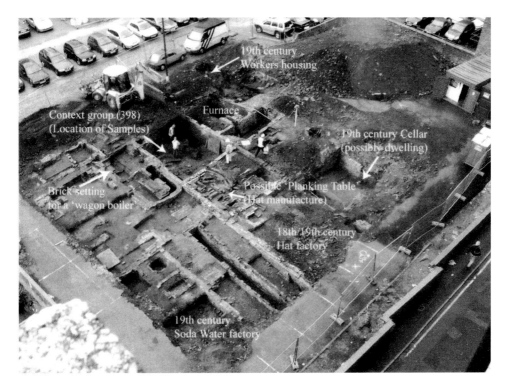

49 The Hardman Street excavations revealed the eighteenth-century hat works built and run by the Bower family, leading Manchester traders. Adjacent to the hat works, to the left, was a soda works for producing bottled sparkling water, established around 1800

According to one tradition it was Miles Bower Sr who laid the foundation stone of the Manchester Infirmary in Piccadilly in 1755 (Axon 1886, 91; Nevell with Grimsditch & Hradil 2007, 7-9).

The remains of their hat factory, including the foundations for a planking stove and two dyeing vats, were excavated in 2002 and comprised several phases of activity beginning in the first quarter of the eighteenth century (50). The dye house was a separate building at the back of the property, whilst the planking shop was in a room at the back of the house.

A surprising amount of the Georgian boom town survives above ground as standing structures. The best known upstanding fragments are St Ann's Church built in 1709-12, the adjacent St Ann's Square laid out in 1720 (Hartwell 2001, 199-202) and King Street, laid out south of the cathedral in the second quarter of the eighteenth century (Hartwell 2001, 162-8). Both St Ann's Square and King Street were high-class residential areas and on Casson and Berry's map of Manchester from the 1740s are shown as having terraced and detached town houses with lines of trees along the roadways. Only King Street retains any eighteenth-century fabric. No. 56, which was built around 1700, retains some original interiors including panelling and plasterwork on the first floor, whilst Nos 35-37 is a five-bay brick-built house that retains much of its original façade, although the

50 These circular brick stoves were to support the dye vats at the hat works and date from the mid eighteenth century

two wings have gone, as has the ground floor interior. It was built in 1736 for Dr Peter Waring, but became a bank in 1772. The best-preserved Georgian town house in the city centre is the brick-built three-storey Cobden House on the corner of Quay Street and Byrom Street. Built in the 1770s by the Byrom family it retains much of its original restrained symmetrical façade and inside has a restored interior that includes a large hallway and grand staircase. These are the only surviving examples of the many detached town houses built by the middle and merchant classes in the eighteenth century, though representations of some of these grand buildings survive as small pictures around Casson and Berry's map. Of the seven churches built in Manchester between 1756 and 1794, none survive. Manchester's increasingly rapid commercial, industrial and urban growth was noted in 1783 by James Ogden who remarked that:

> The large and populous town of Manchester has now excited the attention and curiosity of strangers, on account of its extensive trade and the rapid increase of its buildings with the enlargement of its streets
>
> Ogden 1783

By this date a number of areas were being developed on the eastern and southern edges of the town. In the 1770s, the lands owned by the Legh family between Oldham Street and Great Ancoats Street were laid out, and the Minshull family sold land for building between Piccadilly and the Medlock, including what would later become Portland Street and Princess Street. The Lever estate lands north of Piccadilly were sold off in a piecemeal fashion for development in the 1770s and 1780s. Much of this was sold to one developer, William Stevenson, who laid out a grid of streets focusing upon Stevenson Square. In 1783 the Mosley family sold land in the area that later became Mosley Street and by 1788 the Byrom family had laid out streets in the area between Water Street, Quay Street and Deansgate (Hartwell 2001, 12; Parkinson-Bailey 2000, 8-9).

The area with the greatest concentration of surviving eighteenth-century buildings is that to the north of Piccadilly gardens and east of the cathedral, now known as the Northern Quarter. Within this area there are the remains of dozens of buildings from the second half of the eighteenth century, such as workers' housing, merchants' residences, warehouses, pubs and churches.

Perhaps the most interesting archaeologically are the brick-built vernacular workshop dwellings that can still be found all over this area (*51*). The highest surviving concentration of late eighteenth-century workers' housing lies in that part of the area that was known in this period as the St Paul's District, where 53 examples dating from the period 1750 to 1800 have been recorded and the foundations of several examples excavated. The workshop dwelling was characterised by having three storeys and a cellar, and was usually one bay deep. The upper storey or attic contained a workshop lit by long multi-light windows and the cellar was usually used as a workshop as well. Such workshop dwellings were the counterpart to the rural weaver's cottage, though in fact they allowed all sorts of home-based craftsmen to ply their trades (Roberts 1999, 2).

The character of the thriving mid eighteenth-century merchant and textile manufacturing town before the arrival of the first cotton mill, with its Cotton Exchange of 1729 and Infirmary of 1754-55, is captured in Manchester's first directory published in 1772 (Nevell 2003). Its 1495 entries within the main directory represent a cross-section of Manchester society, though this was only 6.5 per cent of the 23,032 people recorded as living in the town in the following year. The occupations listed within the 1772 directory (Nevell 2003) can be broken down into textiles (29.3 per cent), food retailers (15.3 per cent), retailers (14.8 per cent) and other occupations such as hatting, forging and smithying (13.8 per cent), home-based manufacturing workers (13.2 per cent), those with no occupation listed (9.3 per cent) and warehousemen (4.3 per cent). Although textiles were not overwhelming in their dominance, they did form the largest single grouping, with 439 individuals – just under a third of all the entries – describing themselves as involved in the trade. Within this grouping, the largest entries were for fustian manufacturers (3.9 per cent of the directory), check manufacturers (2.7 per cent) and smallware manufacturers (2.4 per cent). Individually these figures do not reflect the dominance of the fustian sector which accounted for 173 entries or 11.6 per cent of the main directory.

Whilst individual house numbers are not given, the historical geography of this textile industry can be recovered by looking at the distribution of the various branches of the textile trade, manufacturers, weavers and finishers, street by street. The entries referring

51 Nos 36 to 38 Back Turner Street was typical of vernacular workshop dwellings built in eighteenth-century Manchester. Erected around 1760, this building had the distinctive long top floor window which allowed lots of light into the attic workspace.

to textile manufacturers appear to relate to textile merchants involved in the putting-out trade. Their commercial premises can be found all over the centre of the town, with notable concentrations along Cannon Street, the northern end of Deansgate, King Street and Market Street. The location of those involved in textile weaving and calendaring, presumably in domestic workshops, shows that there were two major concentrations. The first was in the Aldport area of Manchester, now the southern third of Deansgate, and the second in the streets around Turner Street in what is now the Northern Quarter. Finally, textile finishers could be found around the fringes of the town in the 1770s, where there was access to plentiful supplies of clean water, principally along the Rivers Irk and Irwell, but also along Shooters Brook on the eastern edge of the town.

THE MERSEY AND IRWELL NAVIGATION AND THE BRIDGEWATER CANAL

As well as witnessing a boom in the domestic-based manufacturing industry, Manchester saw the first phase of its transport revolution during this period, with the establishment of the Mersey and Irwell Navigations' wharf on the River Irwell and the building of the world's first industrial canal from Worsley to Castlefield – the Bridgewater Canal (Nevell 2005) (*52*).

The first purpose-built eighteenth-century waterfront in Manchester lay along the River Irwell west of Water Street (George & Brumhead 2002, 22-3). Attempts to make the rivers Mersey and Irwell navigable were made as early as the 1660s, though none were successful until the passing of the Mersey and Irwell Navigation Act of June 1721. This Act of Parliament formally authorised the navigation of the Upper Mersey and Irwell. In effect these rivers were now classified as canals that acted as an important trade route from Manchester to the port of Liverpool. The new Navigation enabled seagoing vessels of up to 50 tons to sail up the Irwell into Manchester, though the upgrading of the rivers and the building of eight new locks was slow and the Navigation was not opened until 1734. Wharfage facilities were not in place at Manchester until 1735-36 when the new quay was built by Edward Byrom at a cost of £1,200 with a river frontage of 136 yards (George & Brumhead 2002; Hadfield & Biddle 1970, 16-8). In 1755, Salford

52 Manchester's first purpose-built waterfront opened in 1736 at the bottom of Quay Street was built by the Mersey & Irwell Navigation. This view dates from around 1740 and shows a warehouse and a Mersey Flat sailing boat

Old Quay was opened by the Navigation opposite the Manchester Quay in order to secure the Salford trade. The Manchester quay was strategically located to handle much of the town's early trade. Situated at the junction of Water Street and Quay Street, the complex comprised, according to line drawings of 1741 and 1746, a three-storey, L-shaped warehouse with hoists operated by wooden shafting and gearing worked by a horse gin (George & Brumhead 2002), as well as a single-storey range of buildings at right angles to the south and a purpose-built quay.

The first plan of the Navigation's quay in Manchester can be seen on Fothergill's map of Manchester from 1772, which shows a U-shaped arrangement of buildings surrounding a central riverside structure. By this date the land either side of the quay had been built upon and was being used for textile finishing. Green's map of Manchester published in 1794 shows the site in further detail, indicating that the original warehouse had been incorporated into south-eastern corner of the greatly expanded quay buildings. Much of the Navigation's trade was bulk cargo, such as cotton and timber. The purchase of 10 new vessels and improvement works on locks and weirs in 1791 is indicative of the upsurge in trade at that time, as is the incorporation of the Mersey and Irwell Navigation by Act of Parliament in March 1794.

The second significant transport development in Manchester was the building of the Bridgewater Canal and its Castlefield canal basin (53). The reason for the construction of the Bridgewater Canal in the 1760s was the transhipment of coal from the Duke of Bridgewater's collieries in Worsley to Manchester. This canal reduced the transport costs, halving the price of coal in Manchester (Ogden 1783) and its extension to the River Mersey at Runcorn in 1776 halved the cost of transporting raw cotton to Manchester (Kidd 2002, 32). This canal gradually developed into the Mersey and Irwell Navigation Company's greatest rival, the peak of this competition was reached only in the period 1830-44. Prior to 1830, the Bridgewater Canal and the Navigation were limited competitors. The staple of the Bridgewater Canal's trade in the eighteenth century was a mixture of bulk cargo such as coal, cotton, timber and market produce from the great agricultural estates of northern Cheshire. The first market boat to run from Altrincham began in 1770 and in that year carried 2730 tons of goods, whilst the first ran from the Heatley wharf near Lymm in 1786 and carried 1559 tons that year. The importance of this trade is shown in the growth of general purpose warehouses in the Castlefield Canal Basin in the late eighteenth century. The Duke's Warehouse was open by 1771; the Grocer's Warehouse, which was used by Henshall's for market produce, was open from the late 1770s onwards and the Staffordshire Warehouse was built around 1790. The mixed trade the Bridgewater specialised in continued to grow in the early nineteenth century. This was aided by the building of two canal links in this period. The opening of the Rochdale Canal link in 1804 gave the Bridgewater access to the textile trade on the eastern side of Manchester around the suburb of Ancoats, to the coal trade from Ashton-under-Lyne and to the cross-Pennine trade with Yorkshire. The opening of a physical link with the Leeds and Liverpool Canal in 1821 boosted the vegetable trade from Ormskirk.

Archaeologically, the remains of the Bridgewater Canal, its canal basin and associated buildings in Castlefield, are amongst the best known industrial period monuments in

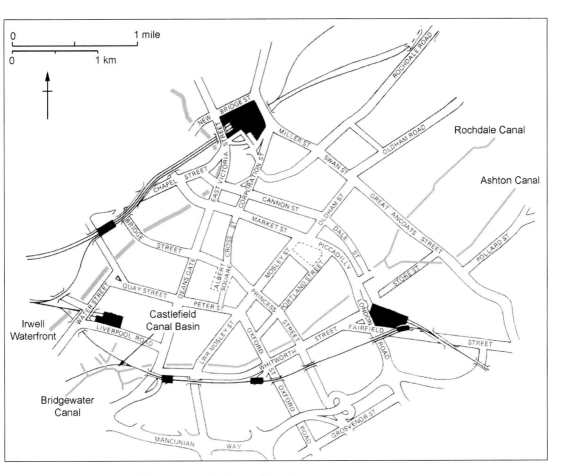

53 The late eighteenth-century canals of central Manchester

Manchester, if not in Britain. The Bridgewater Canal was the first industrial canal, running across watersheds without relying on the existing courses of streams or rivers (*54*). It was built between 1759 and 1765 between Worsley and Castlefield. It was designed to bring domestic coal supplies by boat from the Duke of Bridgewater's colliery at Worsley to the largest market in the North West – Manchester. James Brindley acted as the engineering consultant and John Gilbert as the resident engineer. Two significant engineering problems had to be overcome. The first was the bridging of the River Irwell; this was achieved by building the stone-arched Barton aqueduct, replaced by a hydraulic swing bridge in 1894, across the Manchester Ship Canal (a section of the original aqueduct survives on the western bank of the later ship canal). The second feat of engineering was the construction of the Castlefield canal basin that involved harnessing the waters of the River Medlock and redirecting the river bed via an overflow sluice on the eastern side of Deansgate that took the surplus water via a tunnel to below the Giant's Basin. This was a massive clover-leaf shaped weir at the western end of the canal basin designed to manage the water flow of the basin. This water management system proved problematic and much of it was altered and replaced at the end of the eighteenth century. Archaeological investigations during the 1990s redevelopment of the basin demonstrated that little of the clover leaf weir survived beyond the still visible central siphon and small area of apron surrounding it. However, in 2006 excavations showed that the edge of the apron was defined by a deep, narrow, stone-lined channel that was heavily silt filled, which might go some way towards explaining the specific problems with the system.

The Castlefield canal basin's archaeological importance lies to a large degree in the survival of several early canal warehouses and in its role in the development of this new industrial monument type. Six canal warehouses were built around the Castlefield canal basin between c.1770 and the 1840s, a mixture of company and privately financed structures. These were three warehouses from the late eighteenth century (Duke's, Grocer's and Staffordshire), the Merchant's built in 1825, the Middle Warehouse built around 1831 and Kenworthy's Warehouse built in the 1840s.

Archaeological attention has focused on the two earliest warehouses – the Duke's and the Grocer's – and the first serious archaeological study of these monuments, indeed the first modern industrial archaeology fieldwork undertaken in Manchester, was by Tomlinson. He examined the Grocer's Warehouse, built during the 1770s, during its demolition in 1960 (55). Further study of this monument was undertaken in GMAU in the 1980s ahead of its partial reconstruction, whilst survey work by UMAU in the

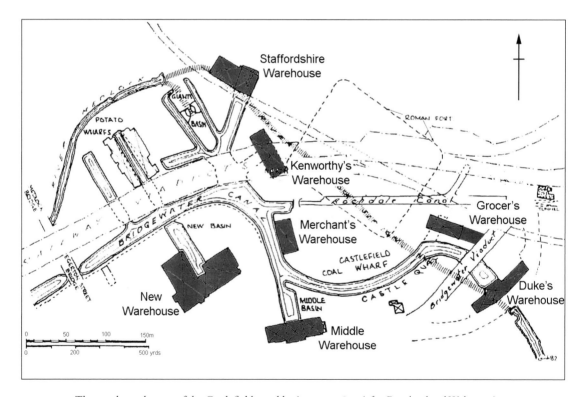

54 The canal warehouses of the Castlefield canal basin, 1770-1840 (after Bromhead and Wyke 1997)

late 1990s demonstrated that the northern and eastern elevations of the final form of the warehouse survived to roof level. The warehouse was a multi-phased structure successively enlarged around 1800 and 1807, culminating in a brick structure five storeys high with two shipping holes and a floor area of around 3888m² divided by a series of transverse brick walls (56). This was more than double the floor area of the original 1770s warehouse (Nevell & Walker 2001, 71).

The Duke's Warehouse was built in the early 1770s and burnt down in 1919. During 1998, the site of the warehouse was partially excavated ahead of redevelopment revealing brick and stone foundations on the northern side of the structure up to 0.5m deep and confirming the irregular final floor plan of the structure. The primary phase was a central square block straddling the River Medlock with two internal shipping holes. This four-storey brick structure had a floor area of around 2024m². Two phases between 1778 and 1785 saw the incorporation of the old fulling mill on the southern bank of the Medlock with the old cottages on the northern bank producing a dog leg or stepped plan form. It was extensively rebuilt after a fire in 1789, producing a warehouse with a floor area of c.5228m². Today only the platform terraced into the northern bank of the Medlock marks the site of the northern third of the warehouse.

Both the Duke's and the Grocer's Warehouses represent the developed form of the canal warehouse. This was an innovative structure combining multiple storeys, split level loading, terracing, internal water-filled canal arms and a hoist system run by water power. Although it owed much to its coastal and urban predecessors this was a unique form

55 The Grocer's Warehouse, seen here partially reconstructed, dates from the early 1770s and along with the nearby Duke's Warehouse of the same date was the earliest canal warehouse in Manchester

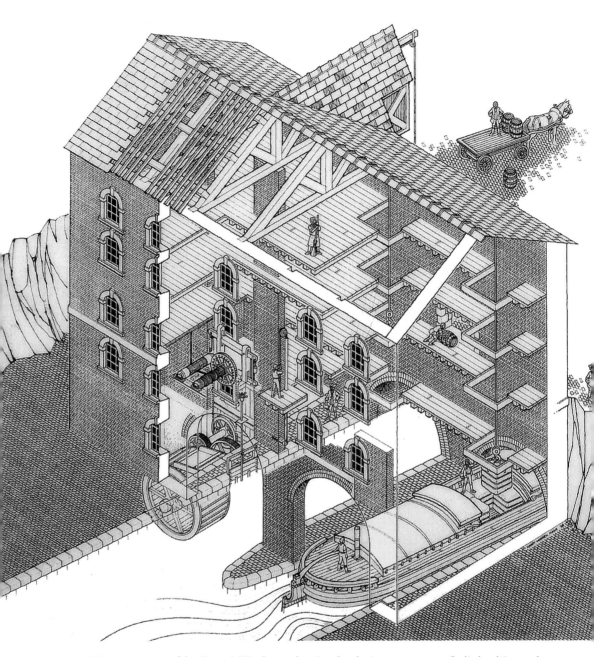

56 Reconstruction of the Grocer's Warehouse showing the classic arrangement of split-level, internal loading and unloading from the covered canal arms

that appears to have been developed specifically in the Castlefield Canal basin of the Bridgewater Canal in the late 1760s and 1770s. The first canal warehouse of this type was almost certainly the Duke's Warehouse. However, the earliest surviving canal warehouse of this classic design is the ruinous Grocers' Warehouse.

It is relatively easy to find antecedents for three of the five major elements of the classic canal warehouse design. Multi-storeyed warehouses had long been in use in urban contexts and during the early and mid eighteenth century many dock facilities around Britain, from Lancaster to London, were being rebuilt using just such buildings (Crowe 1994, 65-7). These structures often used split level loading via external man- or horse-powered hoists attached to the top of the waterside elevation of the structure. In the North West the Mersey and Irwell Navigation Company were amongst the first to build such structures during the redevelopment of their Warrington and Manchester quays, in the 1720s and 1730s respectively (Hadfield & Biddle 1970). One of these structures in particular may have provided the inspiration for the classic canal warehouse design. The Rock House was erected by the Mersey and Irwell Navigation Company in Manchester by 1728. It lay on the eastern bank of the River Irwell, just south of the site of the present Blackfriars Bridge in the area of the Parsonage, where it is shown on S & N Buck's view of the south-western prospect of the town from that year. This building was located on the edge of a sheer cliff above the river, a drop of roughly 15m (Nevell 2003, 35-6). In order to overcome the height difference between the two, a four-storey split level loading warehouse was built flush with the river bank but terraced into the hillside. The river façade had an external hoist system and four storeys, whilst the road side had just two storeys, allowing boats to be unloaded via a jib crane directly into carts at road level (Tomlinson 1961, 130-1).

It was the two final elements of the canal warehouse – the internal water-filled canal arms that brought the canal right into the centre of the structure and a hoist system run by water power – combined with the multi-storey dock and urban warehouse with its split-level loading tradition that made the building type revolutionary. The development of such a bold building may have been as much an accident of geography as the result of industrial inspiration. The topography of the River Medlock through the Castlefield area of Manchester was very similar to that of the Irwell below Manchester Cathedral, with sheer cliffs at a number of points along the river valley between the line of Deansgate and the junction of the River Medlock with the River Irwell. In 1763, Castlefield was chosen by James Brindley as the terminus for the Duke of Bridgewater's new industrial canal that would bring coal from his mines at Worsley into the heart of Manchester. Clearly the height difference between the river and the town, approximately 7.7m (25ft) would be a problem when unloading the coal from the Duke's mines. The Castlefield basin of the Bridgewater Canal was opened in the summer of 1765 (Malet 1977, 99; Tomlinson 1961, 132-3), but lacked any warehouse facilities, so initially coals were hauled by carts up a steep routeway cut into the northern terrace of the River Medlock. By 1769, a number of cottages had been converted into warehouses on the northern bank of the River Medlock where it was crossed by the line of Deansgate and these are shown on Young's map of the Castlefield Basin published in 1770 (Tomlinson 1961, 139-40). As Tomlinson has detailed, Young's contemporary description of the canal basin shows that Brindley had something more ambitious in mind as a way of overcoming the 7.7m height difference between river and town. No doubt using the experience he had gained in building the underground network of canals at the Worsley coal mines (Aldred 1988; Boucher 1968; Malet 1977) Brindley built a brick-arched tunnel that ran from the northern side of the Medlock northwards below the line of the modern Castle Street, from which level a shaft was sunk and a swivel crane used to haul 8cwt boxes of coal directly from the canal boats to the roadway. Power was provide by a 30ft-diameter waterwheel which turned a wooden cylinder carrying a rope for operating the crane, whilst a sluice controlled a flow of water from the underground canal so that it passed through a rock-cut channel to drive the waterwheel (Tomlinson 1961, 140). Here were the two missing elements of the classic canal warehouse design, the covered canal arm and the water-powered hoist system. The great leap of linking these and the split level dock warehouse in one structure must have been made by James Brindley himself (Nevell 2003, 36-7).

Thus, the classic canal warehouse with its distinctive shipping holes, water-powered hoist system, split level loading, multiple storeys and terraced location can be seen to be the creation of the topography and commercial needs of the River Irwell frontage and the Castlefield Canal basin during the mid eighteenth century.

MANCHESTER'S FIRST TEXTILE MILLS

The evidence for workshop dwellings, transport and warehousing shows Manchester had emerged as a manufacturing, marketing and redistribution centre of provincial importance by the 1770s. Yet the expansion of the town did not slow, but increased in rate during the last 20 years of the eighteenth century, when there was an unprecedented growth in industrial activity and the population and physical extent of Manchester more than doubled. This coincided with the building of more than 33 water- and steam-powered textile mills within the city and turned Manchester into the greatest textile mill town in the Britain (57).

The first cotton spinning mill in Manchester was built in the years 1781-82 on Shude Hill and fittingly it was built by Richard Arkwright and four partners, William Bricklebank, John Simpson, Samuel Simpson and John Whittenbury. However, this was 12 years after Arkwright first patented the water-frame, a water-powered cotton spinning machine, and until 1781 there was seemingly no indication that Manchester would become the heart of the factory-based cotton spinning manufacturing trade. Indeed, prior to 1781, the largest textile mill towns in north-west England were Congleton, Macclesfield and Stockport, whilst the heart of the factory-based cotton spinning industry was the Derwent Valley in Derbyshire.

Arkwright's Manchester mill contained water-frame cotton spinning machines and although there are no direct figures to indicate the cost of building and equipping the structure, in 1784, when Arkwright sold his share to his son, it was insured for £3,000 and the machinery for another £1,000, a figure which rose to £5,000 the following year (Champness 2004) (58). The site was destroyed in the Manchester Blitz of 1940 and has since been used as a car park, but in September 2005 the Channel 4 archaeology programme *Time Team*, with the assistance of the University of Manchester, undertook

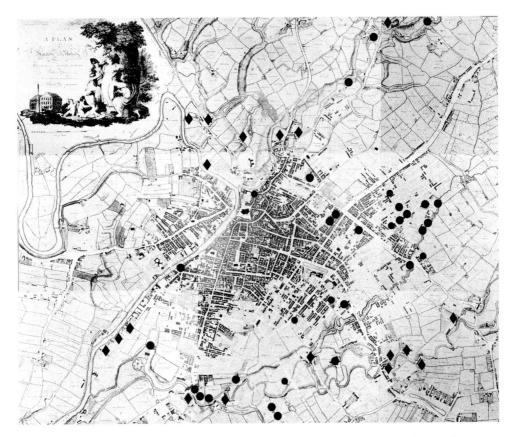

57 The distribution of Manchester's textile factories by 1800. The base-map is Green's map of Manchester published in 1794. Key: dots = cotton spinning factories; diamonds = finishing works

the first excavations on this iconic site. This established that the mill was 52.2m (171ft) long, one of the longest of the mills Arkwright built, 12m (39ft) wide, an exceptional width for any Arkwright-style mill (Chapmen 1981), and was originally five storeys high, with wooden floors supported by a central row of narrow cruciform cast iron columns on each floor (59). The massive scale of this structure was a measure of Manchester's importance as a cotton manufacturing town. The excavations also highlighted several other unusual features of the mill's layout including the large width of the mill, a centrally placed square brick-lined shaft adjacent to the inside of the north-western mill wall and close by an internal wheel pit.

Contemporary accounts record that Arkwright's Mill was the first in Manchester to use steam-power (Chaloner 1955, 90-1) and there is some evidence to suggest that Arkwright tried initially to run his water-frames directly from an atmospheric steam engine (Aspin 2003, 72-3). The local historian James Ogden wrote in 1782 that

Mr Arkwright's machines are setting to work by a steam engine, for carding and spinning cotton. The erection of the mill chimney attracts crowds daily, its height being a source of wonder and not a little misgiving. The mill was turned by water-power, the water being obtained from Shudehill pits, while the engine was used to pump water to a higher level

Ogden 1783

This comment is somewhat contradictory, but does suggest that some of the mill machinery may originally have been powered by steam. There is some correspondence between Arkwright and James Watt on the matter from the early 1780s (Aspin 2003,

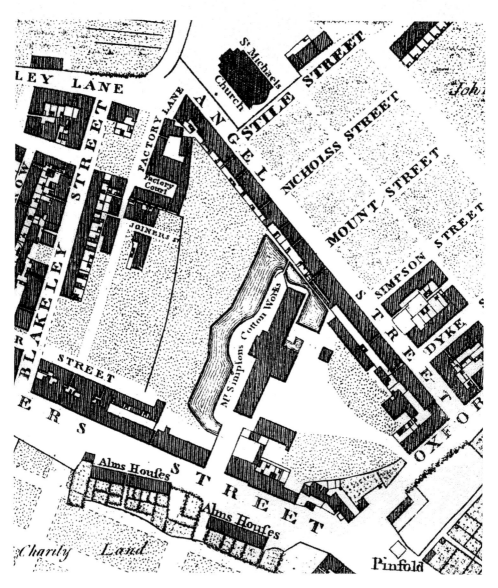

58 The plan of Arkwright's Mill, Manchester's first cotton mill, as shown on Green's 1794 map of Manchester. Here the mill is called Simpson's Mill, after Arkwright's son-in-law who took over the running of the mill in the mid-1780s

59 The 2005 *Time Team* excavations on Arkwright's Mill located the middle of the mill where the 1780s wheelpit and engine house lay

72). According to the Boulton and Watt papers, the first mill engine at Arkwright's Mill was an atmospheric engine designed by Thomas Hunt (Tann 1979). Hunt specialised in producing atmospheric steam engines with a crank and flywheel. A handbill from 1783 claimed that Thomas Hunt of London had erected 22 such rotary steam engines, including two for Richard Arkwright in Manchester (Birmingham Central Library, Boulton and Watt MSS, Muirhead IV, Misc.). It is thus possible that one of these engines ran some of the machinery at Arkwright's Mill on Shudehill. Whilst the *Time Team* excavations did not positively identify the location of this original atmospheric steam engine, the brick square pit, which was 2.2m by 2m in plan and at least 1.36m deep, is a strange primary feature whose function is unclear (60). It is possible, but not certain, that it may have been associated with this engine and may represent the cylinder pit of the original steam engine. The rectangular walls that ran above this pit and across the width of the mill appear to be later.

Nearby was an internal wheel pit, which is shown on a Boulton and Watt drawing of 1789 entitled 'Messrs John & Saml Simpson, Brown Street, Manchester. Feb'y 1789' (Champness 2004) and was 2.4m wide and more than 3m deep. This wheel pit appears to have been a secondary feature since it was only roughly keyed in to the outer mill wall at its north-eastern corner. It would suggest that the experiment with the Hunt engine failed very rapidly, which may account for Ogden's confusing account noted

60 This rectangular structure in the middle of the mill may have been the site of the 1781 steam engine

above. Contemporary documents indicate that the wheel had a diameter of 30ft (9m) by 8ft (2.4m) with two upright line shafts aligned with the central shaft of the water wheel but positioned roughly 3m and 5m from the eastern wall of the mill. Presumably the higher and lower reservoirs are also contemporary with the wheel pit. The wheel pit and these reservoirs are shown for the first time on Laurent's map on Manchester, which was published in 1789.

Whatever the precise arrangements of the original power system, by 1789 the mill was run by water and it seems highly likely that the water supply for the mill came from a leat drawn from nearby ponds known as the Shude Hill Pitts on Swan Street, which in their turn were fed directly from the River Tib. This was a closed system, since the water was not lost, but recycled by being pumped from the lower reservoir to the west of mill back uphill to a small square header reservoir north-east of the mill using an atmospheric steam engine (*61*). Precisely how the water got on to the wheel is unclear but the Boulton and Watt drawing of 1789 shows a beam engine with a 64in cylinder at its eastern end and at its western end two 31in pumps opposite the water wheel. It is thus tempting to suggest that the water may have been pumped directly onto the wheel, but this point remains unclear (*62*).

During the 1780s at least 10 more mills were built in Manchester and of these, all except one of the primary phase factory buildings appear to have been water-powered. On the southern banks of the River Irk on Long Millgate, William Edge built a cotton spinning mill, Mill Hill Mill, in 1783. Garratt Mill on the River Medlock, which had been built as a silk spinning mill in 1760 and was Manchester's first purpose-built textile mill, was converted by Joseph Thackery, John Whitehead and Joseph Ryder to cotton spinning in 1783. In 1786, James Entwistle built a three-storey cotton spinning mill in Ancoats along Shooters Brook, the first in this suburb of Manchester (Aspin 2003, 453-455). By 1788, a further six water-powered mills had been built: Commercial Street Mill, Gaythorne Mill and Wood Mill, all on the River Medlock; Travis' Mill on the Irk, and New Islington Mill and Salvin's Factory on Shooters Brook in the Ancoats suburb (Chapman 1981; Nevell 2003, 40).

61 The earliest image of Arkwright's Mill is this view from a view of Manchester from the north-west published in 1795 by John Aikin. It shows the north-western elevation with, behind, a chimney

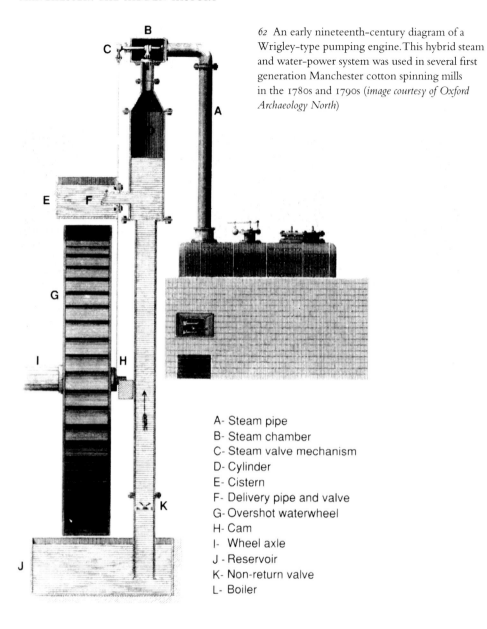

62 An early nineteenth-century diagram of a Wrigley-type pumping engine. This hybrid steam and water-power system was used in several first generation Manchester cotton spinning mills in the 1780s and 1790s (*image courtesy of Oxford Archaeology North*)

A- Steam pipe
B- Steam chamber
C- Steam valve mechanism
D- Cylinder
E- Cistern
F- Delivery pipe and valve
G- Overshot waterwheel
H- Cam
I- Wheel axle
J - Reservoir
K- Non-return valve
L- Boiler

These latter two sites were excavated in 2005. The excavations at New Islington Mill indicated that the factory was 30m long and 15.25m wide and aligned with its eastern gable to the brook (63). The power house was at this end of the mill structure. The original wheel pit appears to have been largely destroyed by the insertion of a beam engine on the same site at the end of the 1790s, although a large culvert was excavated running underneath the steam engine house (Miller & Wild 2007, 41-2). The remains of Salvin's Factory, a smaller brick structure of 22m by 11m, straddled the brook but, as at New Islington, the evidence for the primary water power system was very fragmentary and comprised only the remains of a large culvert, which ran along

63 Excavations on the site of New Islington Mill revealed the remains of a Wrigley-type pumping system with a water wheel (centre)

the eastern bank of the brook towards the eastern end of the mill (Miller & Wild 2007, 35-6). Around 1791, documentary evidence indicates that a steam-powered pumping engine was installed so as to guarantee a constant supply of water for the wheel (Hills 1970, 141). This seems to have been a steam engine built by the local Manchester engineer Joshua Wrigley, producing roughly 20hp that serviced a water wheel of 12ft in diameter (3.66m). Unfortunately, neither the wheel pit nor the engine house survived at Salvin's Factory, although a secondary culvert was located at the eastern end of the mill that appears to have been associated with this phase of the mill (Miller & Wild 2007, 36). Wrigley's system was a development of a pumping engine patented by Thomas Savery in 1698 that comprised a pair of vessels into which steam was admitted alternately. The steam was condensed in turn in each vessel creating a partial vacuum which forced water into one and then the other vessel producing the pumping action (Farey 1827, 99). Wrigley adapted this pump, increasing the power by adding a wagon boiler and arranging the mechanism so that the water was pumped by atmospheric pressure from a lower reservoir to a higher reservoir from where it fell directly onto a wheel, thereby creating an overshot waterwheel. As Miller and Wild have noted 'it was cheap to build as it did not require the precision engineering demanded by machines comprising a piston and accurately bored cylinder, and no premiums were charged for its use' (Miller & Wild 2007, 45).

The Wrigley system of steam pumping engine and waterwheel provided, at £200 in 1790 for the whole system (Tann 1979, 122), a cheap technological bridge between the water-powered water-frames developed by Richard Arkwright and the new rotary beam engine that came to power the mule-spinning machine, which later typified the Manchester textile mill. Other Manchester mills known to have employed this system in the late eighteenth century include Garratt Mill in 1784 and possibly Arkwright's Mill after 1783 (Hills 1970). When James Watt Jr visited Manchester in March 1791 he noted that Wrigley had 'orders for 13 engines for this town and neighbourhood, all of them intended for working cotton machinery of one kind or other' (Musson & Robinson 1969, 403). Nor was this arrangement to be found only in Manchester; in Yorkshire at least 35 mill sites were using pumping engines by 1800 (Giles & Goodall 1992, 133). So far the only excavated Wrigley system is at New Islington Mill, where a steam pumping engine and water wheel arrangement was installed at the surprisingly late date of 1815-19; precisely what is was running is unclear (Miller & Wild 2007, 49). The power generated by such a system was limited and the design had been superseded in the later 1790s by the continued development of the steam-powered rotary beam engine.

By the late 1780s most of the best locations for water-powered textile mill sites along the Irk, Medlock and Shooters Brook had been used, either for Arkwright-style mills or by the booming textile finishing industry. By 1794 there were 20 textile finishing works within the township of Manchester, making the town the leading area in the finishing sector (Nevell 2003, 41-2; Nevell, Connelly, Hradil & Stockley 2003). If Manchester's mills were to continue to expand they needed to find a way of powering the mill that dispensed with the waterwheel. The answer lay in the steam engine developed by Matthew Boulton and Isaac Watt. Boulton and Watt had patented the rotary (sun and plant), double-action, reciprocating steam engine in 1785. In 1786 steam power was used successfully to spin cotton at Papplewick Mill in Nottinghamshire where just such a rotating engine was installed to supplement the existing water-powered transmission system (Palmer & Neaverson 1998, 73). Soon after, in 1789, the first purpose-built steam-powered mill in Manchester, where the engine actually ran the spinning machinery, was erected by Peter Drinkwater (Williams with Farnie 1992). Drinkwater was one of the Manchester fustian putting-out merchants who made the transition to cotton mill owner. During the 1770s he was a fustian manufacturer with commercial premises including a warehouse in King Street, a town house in Spring Gardens and extensive overseas interests. During the late 1780s he began investing some of the capital he had accumulated in cotton spinning mills, first in a water-powered mill in Northwich and then in 1789 in Manchester, with the construction of the four-storey, brick-built Piccadilly Mill on Auburn Street. By the early 1790s it employed around 500 people (Chaloner 1955, 85-93, 162-3). This was powered by an 8hp Boulton and Watt rotary beam engine (the original drawings for which can still be seen in the company's archives at Birmingham), installed and working by 1 May 1790 and immediately increasing the output of his business 30-fold (Chaloner 1955, 87-90). A fragment of the south-eastern brick wall of this mill, surviving up to 13 courses high, was identified in excavations by Oxford Archaeology North in 2004, though the excavators did not have the opportunity to locate the engine house.

Drinkwater's Piccadilly Mill is important for its use of mule spinning machines rather than water-frames. Mule spinning was developed by Samuel Crompton in 1779. This was a combination of the jenny and the water frame that used the bare spindle-spinning of the former and the drafting rollers of the latter to produce a very fine, hard-twisted yarn suitable for warps and able to match the fine muslin fabrics of India (Benson 1983, 15). Originally hand-powered with just 48 spindles, the mule was rapidly developed by mill-owners (it was not patented by Crompton much to his disadvantage) so that by 1790 mules with 150 spindles were common and by 1800 a semi-automatic version held 400 spindles. This version of the mule was designed to be partially power-driven so that the movement of the carriage and the twisting, stretching and drawing out of the yarn could be water or steam driven, although backing-off and winding still had to be done by hand (Jones 1996, 249). The attraction to the Manchester textile merchants of the late 1780s and early 1790s was threefold: it was not a patented design, it could be hand- or steam-powered and it produced a fine, strong yarn which could be used for the warp and weft, unlike the water-frame which only produced coarse yarn suitable for the warp.

The first occurrence of mule spinning in Manchester is alluded to in an advertisement in the *Manchester Mercury* on the 21 March 1786, when some mules were offered for sale (Little 2007, 14). Since mule spinning would dominate Lancashire's cotton spinning industry until its collapse in the mid twentieth century, this was a revolutionary moment. By the early 1790s, workshops and mills that were suitable for mule spinning were being erected by speculators. One such is recorded in an advertisement in the *Manchester Mercury* of 11 September 1792 which offered 'three rooms, 17 yards by 14, very convenient, for spinning jennies or mules … situated near Newton Lane'. Steve Little has demonstrated that during this period there was an initial hand-powered phase of both mule and jenny production, some of which was in purpose-built small-scale factories and some of which must have taken place in the vernacular workshops common to northern Manchester at this time (Little 2007, 15-16).

This phase was short-lived, for the application of steam power to the mule was perfected in the early 1790s in Manchester. During this decade almost all of the 22 mills known to have been built in the town were steam-powered and ran mule spinning machines. A significant number of these new steam-powered mills lay in the new industrial suburb of Ancoats, which saw 10 mills built in this decade (Miller & Wild 2007, 28), nearly half of the total known to have been erected in this period. Many of these new factories were built by speculators who provided the premises and steam power, but let the floors of the mill to individuals and companies. This was known as the 'room and power' system. Mills arranged in this way included Ancoats Bridge Mill, built in 1791, Mr Lane's Factory, built in 1793 (with four tenants by 1797) and Sedgewick's Mill built in 1794 (Little 2007, 19, 21). Salvin's Factory was also used as a room and power mill and was the first home of the company founded by James McConnel and John Kennedy – one of the great early nineteenth-century Manchester cotton spinning firms (Williams with Farnie 1992, 51), as was New Islington Mill, (Miller & Wild 2007, 42). Elsewhere within Manchester, Bridge Street Mill built close to the River Irwell in 1791, is also recorded as a room and power mill.

The only one of the eighteenth-century steam-powered cotton mills to survive is Adam and George Murray's Old Mill on the Rochdale Canal in Ancoats, which was erected in 1798, but expanded into a much larger complex by 1806 (Miller & Wild 2007). The development of this complex will be discussed in further detail in the next chapter. Murray's Old Mill came to typify the early nineteenth-century Manchester cotton factory; it was a narrow, eight-storey, brick-built structure of 32m by 11m with 11 bays located on the side of a canal, a 12hp beam engine powering carding machines and spinning mules. It employed hundreds of workers on regular hours for payment by the piece.

'THE GREATEST MERE VILLAGE IN ENGLAND'

The eighteenth century is the key transitional period in Manchester's archaeology and history, for it marks the emergence of the town as an urban centre of provincial importance and as the dominant commercial and manufacturing force in the cotton industry. The radical changes to the town's size and economic base are still reflected in the surviving street pattern and buildings from this period within the city centre, whilst late twentieth-century and early twenty-first-century redevelopment has allowed archaeologists for the first time to study the housing, small-scale industries and mills of this Georgian boom town. The scale of the eighteenth-century town is impressive, but it was to be dwarfed by Manchester blossoming as the world's first industrial city during the first half of the nineteenth century.

CHAPTER 5

THE WORLD'S FIRST INDUSTRIAL CITY

THE ARCHAEOLOGY OF NINETEENTH–CENTURY MANCHESTER

Visitors to Manchester in the first half of the nineteenth century were all astonished by the city's industrial growth. Johann Georg May, a German civil servant and factory commissioner sent to England by the Prussian government to study British industry, and perhaps to spy, visited Manchester in 1814. He wrote:

> Manchester is famous throughout the world as the centre of cotton manufacture … There are hundreds of factories … which tower up to five and six storeys in height. Huge chimneys at the side of these buildings belch forth black coal vapours and this tells us that powerful steam engines are used. The clouds of coal vapour can be viewed afar. The houses are blackened by it.
>
> Bradshaw 1987, 25

Another German, the Frankfurt merchant Johann Heinrich Meidinger, travelled to Britain a few years later, visiting the town in 1820, but was less impressed:

> Manchester is a sprawling town with few beautiful streets and buildings – mostly nothing else apart from warehouses and factories. Among the workers one sees a large number of pale and poorly-dressed people who live on buttermilk, oatcakes and potatoes
>
> Bradshaw 1987, 30

This pattern of divided opinions on the character and importance of Manchester was a feature of much of the social commentary on the city for the rest of the century, but everyone seemed to agree that Manchester's industrial growth was unprecedented and extraordinary.

This industrial growth continued to be led by the cotton spinning industry. By 1799 over 33 textile mills housing 51 firms had been built within the city centre, but by 1816 this number had grown to 86 steam-powered cotton spinning mills (McNeil & Nevell 2000; Williams with Farnie 1992, 19). The rapid factory-based industrialisation of the late eighteenth and early nineteenth century coincided with a phenomenal rise in population, the city nearly doubling its size from 75,281 to 126,066 between 1801 and 1821 and then more than doubling by 1851, when there were 303,382 people within the new borough (Hartwell 2001, 17) (*64*). This was the creation of the world's first industrial city; a dynamic manufacturing, commercial and marketing urban centre with a huge landless urban tenantry, which the Victorians nick-named 'Cottonopolis'.

These figures capture some, but by no means all, of the nature of the growth of nineteenth-century Manchester and characterise the two main types of site that have been surveyed and excavated by archaeologists within the city since the late 1980s: houses and mills. This chapter will focus upon the archaeological remains of nineteenth-century industrialisation in the form of manufacturing industry and transport, whilst Chapter 6 looks at the progress of urbanisation through the physical remains of housing within the late Georgian and Victorian city.

ANCOATS AND THE COTTON MILLS OF MANCHESTER

One of the most extraordinary features of the industrial revolution in Britain was the growth of a manufacturing industry in Lancashire based upon a plant – cotton – grown thousands of miles away in northern America and Egypt, that had to be imported, spun and woven in the surrounding countryside and then transported to the London market.

64 An aerial view from the mid 1980s of the textile mills in the northern part of Ancoats. Those of McConnel & Kennedy and A & G Murray line the northern side of the canal. (*Copyright GMAU/English Heritage*)

That this should be economically viable is testament to the efficacy of the industrialisation process. By 1800, Manchester had become the leading cotton spinning manufacturing centre in Lancashire, and thus Britain and the world. This was fuelled both by the ever-increasing demand for cheap, light-weight cottons that could be dyed, printed and cut to all sorts of fashionable styles, and the convergence of technological innovations and mercantile capital within this one town.

The physical expression of this industrialisation, based around mechanised spinning and later the weaving of cotton, was the mill; there are more than 172 textile mill sites in Manchester built between the establishment of the first factory in 1781 (Arkwright's Mill on Miller Street) and the last mill in 1924 (in Miles Platting). Less than 30 mills survived within Manchester into the early twenty-first century, and these are not representative of the chronological spread, construction and motive power of the Manchester mills as a whole. However, excavation work has begun to remedy this accident of survival.

The first generation of late eighteenth-century cotton spinning mills in Manchester were mainly distributed to the north-east, south-east and south of the town along the rivers Irk, Tib and Medlock. These were mainly water-powered mills, but there were also horse-driven factories and handloom weaving factories (Williams with Farnie 1992, 48-53).

By the mid 1790s, this distribution pattern was starting to change, as was the scale and power of the mills themselves. The development of reliable steam engines freed the mill from the need to be close to water, though water was still needed for the boilers that supplied the engines with steam. The district where this transition began was Ancoats. For much of the eighteenth century this was a rural area north-east of Oldham Road and Piccadilly. By the early 1790s, urban Manchester had reached as far north-east as Great Ancoats Street. The completion of the Rochdale Canal in 1804 added to the attractions of Ancoats for the early mill builders; raw cotton and coal could be transported by canal and all the local mills used canal water for their steam plant. Furthermore, a network of canal arms and basins were constructed to link these industrial sites to the main canal. The first textile mill within the Ancoats area was probably Salvin's Factory, a water-powered cotton spinning mill on Shooters Brook in production by 1788. Several other water-powered mills were built on Shooters Brook over the next few years but the brook's water supply was never plentiful and became increasingly irregular as more water was extracted, leading to the innovation of steam pumping water directly onto the water wheels. The first true steam-powered mill in Ancoats may have been Ancoats Bridge Mill built in 1791 (Miller & Wild 2007, 28), but the site that came to symbolise Ancoats' and Manchester's steam-powered cotton spinning factory revolution was the Murray's Mill complex, begun in 1798 and the subject of recent and extensive restoration and archaeological survey.

The earliest and largest part of the Murray's Mills site, bounded by Murray Street to the west and Bengal Street to the east, was built in three phases between 1798 and 1806 (65). It is now the oldest extant mill in Manchester (Williams with Farnie 1992, 159-63). On Redhill Street is Old Mill (the Phase 1 building built between 1798 and 1801). Attached to the east is Decker Mill (the Phase 2 part of the complex built between 1801 and 1804) which necessitated the construction of a new engine house and power

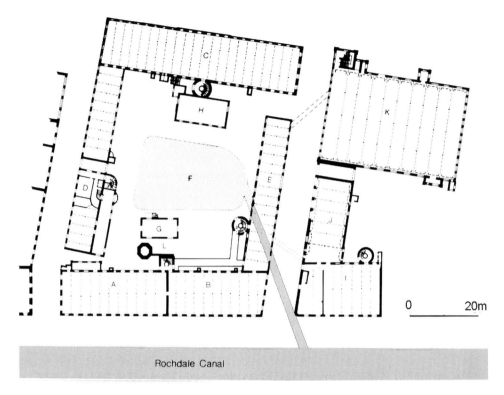

65 A plan of the Murrays Mill complex. Key – A: Old Mill; B: Decker Mill; C: New Mill; D: Murray St block; E: Bengal St block; F: canal basin; G: engine house; H: engine house; I: Doubling Mill; J: Fireproof Mill; K: New Little Mill; L: site of 1802 engine house (*Copyright GMAU/English Heritage*)

transmission system for the Old Mill. The New Mill on Jersey Street and two narrower blocks known as the Murray Street Block and the Bengal Street Block completed the courtyard complex (Phase 3, 1804-17; Miller & Wild 2007, 95-116). These earliest phases of construction, and the history of A & G Murray Limited, reflect a well documented sequence of booms and slumps in the cotton trade between c.1790 and c.1820, the period when Manchester emerged as a major industrial and commercial centre.

Murray's Mills was the largest and one of the most innovative mill complexes in Manchester. Not only did it make extensive use of steam power in buildings, some of which were eight storeys high, but the four multi-storey blocks were built around an enclosed canal basin linked to the Rochdale Canal by a tunnel running beneath Union Street. The addition of this canal basin after the Rochdale Canal opened past the mill in 1804 foreshadowed one of the characteristic features of later mill location in Manchester; access to an adjacent canal arm. The spinning blocks themselves had timber floors supported by cast iron columns of cruciform cross-section and the two larger blocks (Old and Decker Mills and New Mill) were powered by separate Boulton and Watt beam engines via centrally placed upright shafts.

1 A 1978 reconstruction of Roman Manchester and its vicus looking north-east across the River Medlock in the late second century. Image courtesy of The Manchester Museum, University of Manchester

2 An aerial view of the ridge on which the Mellor hillfort sits. This is one of just a handful of Iron Age settlements known within the city region

3 The western elevation of Baguley Hall, one of the oldest buildings within the city. The medieval open hall lies in the centre where the timber-framing can be seen

4 The northern surviving arch of Hanging Bridge, the fourteenth- and fifteenth-century stone bridge across Hanging Ditch

5   The fifteenth-century great hall at Chetham's college. Along with the Cathedral and Hanging Bridge this is the only element of Early Medieval Manchester which is still above the ground

6   Hough Hall in Moston, to the north of the city centre, is one of a number of late medieval and sixteenth-century timber-framed halls to survive within Manchester

8 (above) The foundations of the Lock Keeper's Cottage and the site of a jib crane (the circular area in the centre of the photograph) after excavation work at St George's Island, Hulme Lock, on the Bridgewater Canal

7 (left) The excavated remains of the 1830s engine house at the western end of the 1830 Railway Warehouse off Liverpool Road in Castlefield

9 The Lower Byrom Street railway warehouse was built in the 1880s as the final element of the Liverpool Road Station complex. It is now part of the Museum of Science and Industry in Manchester

10 (right) Late nineteenth- and early twentieth-century textile warehouses along the Rochdale Canal near Princess Street

11 An aerial view of Manchester looking east across the city. Central Station with its wide arched roof can be seen in the middle distance to the right. Since this view was taken in the mid-1990s this sky line has radically altered with the centre of the city having undergone a prolonged period of redevelopment including the erection of a number of tall buildings

Whilst the spinning blocks from Phases 1 to 3 survive, the 1798 12hp steam engine located on the eastern gable of the Old Mill was removed when Decker Mill was built. The new 1801 engine house on the northern side of the enlarged mill has been largely destroyed by the building of an economiser on the site in the late nineteenth century. Almost the complete northern elevation of the 1801 engine house has survived. This contains fragments of the original structure associated with the 40hp steam engine including sandstone blocks to support the frame, or entablature, around the top of the beam engine, a sandstone axle mounting and two blocked arched windows. The northern wall of the external stair tower contains a timber lintel or sole plate that supports a cast iron bearing box that housed the 1801 drive shaft running into the mill via this stair tower. In bay three of Old Mill and bay 18 of Decker Mill, cast iron fittings and empty sockets in many places mark the original position of the two vertical drive shafts that ran them and the branching horizontal line shafting arrangement, from which the belts drove the cotton spinning mule machinery on the upper floors.

The New Mill block built along the southern side of Jersey Street in 1804-06 was an innovative structure. It matched the height of Old Mill and Decker Mill, at eight storeys, but was longer and wider than both (195ft by 46ft or 59.5m by 14m). It had a total floor area of 6664m², more than the combined floor areas of Old Mill (3328m²) and Decker Mill (3204m²). It was built as a single unit and was the largest single spinning factory so far erected in Manchester. The engine house, which still survives and is the earliest engine house in the city, contained a 45hp engine (the stone foundations for which were found during renovation work) and a square chimney, which again is the earliest to survive in the city. The mill featured the first attested circular stair tower in a Manchester mill. Remains of the power distribution system were not as extensive as those for Old Mill and Decker Mill, but a framing for the vertical drive shaft does survive on the fourth floor in bay 10, one of four that rose through the mill and ran the horizontal line shafting and belt drive system. In the northern elevation of the mill on the fourth floor were cut-out wall sections. They had the profile of the end of a spinning mule and show that the mules were arranged in pairs, one per bay, across the whole width of the mill throughout each spinning floor. This is the earliest archaeological evidence for spinning machine arrangements in the city (Miller & Wild 2007, 108-13).

Another feature of New Mill, Decker Mill and Old Mill was the occurrence of Baltic timber shipping marks on some of the major transverse wooden beams supporting the ceilings. These were quality control marks inscribed on pine timbers either on the dockside in Scandinavia before shipping or when the timbers reached Britain. Such timbers were used in these mills because of their length; some were up to 46ft (14m) long, which was longer than any available local oak supplies, whilst being lighter and almost as strong (Miller & Wild 2007, 96-107).

The result of this sustained period of mill building was the largest cotton spinning mill complex in Manchester, employing an unprecedented number of mill hands and mule spindles. This is reflected in an insurance valuation of 1809 covering 65 Manchester cotton factories. The average mill value was £3,668, but Murray's were valued at £20,456 and McConnel & Kennedys' at £18,153 (Daniels 1915). Of the 76 Manchester firms covered in Crompton's census of mule spindleage in 1811, McConnel & Kennedy had 85,000 spindles, Murray's 84,300 and the next largest firm had 48,300 spindles; the majority of Manchester firms were far smaller. By 1815 Murray's employed 1215 hands, McConnel & Kennedy 1020 and the next largest, Houldsworth's Mill, 622 hands. This appears to have been the peak of the firm's industrial significance within the Manchester cotton spinning industry and though new spinning blocks were added in 1819 (Little Mill) and around 1842 (Doubling Mill and Fireproof Mill), McConnel & Kennedy's cotton spinning complex had overtaken Murray's both in size, workforce and mule spindles by 1826. Mule spindleage at McConnel and Kennedy's complex reached 124,848 in that year, while the number of employees at this site peaked at 1590 in 1836. Murray's workforce had dropped to 850 operatives in 1833. By this date the Murray's example of a steam-powered, multi-storey, courtyard cotton spinning factory with access to the canal system had been copied by many other cotton spinning firms throughout the country and not just in Manchester.

By the 1820s, textile mills could be found across Manchester, though the majority were in two main areas – Ancoats and the Chorlton-on-Medlock district (McNeil & Nevell 2000). The Chorlton was an area of Manchester that became incorporated within the town in 1838, when Manchester became a borough (Kidd 2002, 68) (66). Its brief existence as a separate suburb from the 1790s has a lasting monument in the façade of the Chorlton-on-Medlock town hall and dispensary, a grand classical building on

66 Aerial view of the early nineteenth-century mills along Cambridge Street in Chorlton-on-Medlock. To the centre left is Chorlton New Mill. A two-storey weaving mill lay behind this mill

the southern side of Grosvenor Square, one of the earliest middle class housing areas in the city (Hartwell 2001, 132-3). This early middle class suburb was rapidly overtaken by industrial buildings, such as the important grouping of six textile mills along Cambridge Street spanning the period 1795 to 1851. The earliest mill in this area is the five-storey, steam-powered Chorlton Old Mill, erected in 1795 for Robert Owen of New Lanark fame, but almost completely rebuilt in the 1830s. Immediately north is the oldest fireproof mill in Manchester, Chorlton New Mill built by the Birley family (Williams with Farnie 1992, 158-9). This has several features which became obsolete in mid nineteenth-century mill design, thus making it a transitional structure. The eight-storey Cambridge Street wing dates from 1813-15 and contains brick barrel vaulting for fireproofing supported by narrow cast iron beams and three rows of cylindrical cast iron columns. The original internal engine house, for a 100hp engine, lay at the northern end and was separated from the rest of the complex by a substantial cross-wall, a feature that became common in mills with internal engine houses. It was lit by gas from its own internal gas retorts and holders located in the basement, and circulated around the mill through the hollow centres of the cast iron columns supporting the floors. Both were features seldom found in later mills. The six-storey 1818 wing that fronts Hulme Street was fireproof in construction and originally was run by a spur of line-shafting from the 1813-15 engine, although it later had its own external engine house for a large beam engine of around 100hp, which still survived intact as late as 2002. In 1829 a large two-storey, steam-powered weaving shed, capable of housing 600 looms, was added to the rear of the mill along the bank of the River Medlock. At the time this was the largest single weaving shed in Lancashire, though the two-storey design was seldom followed thereafter. The foundations of this weaving shed still form the southern side of the Medlock at this point. Chorlton New Mill was one of the first mills in Manchester to be converted into a combined (spinning and weaving) mill. The 1845 block on the corner of the two streets is a six-storey structure with a large engine house that held a double-beam engine capable of delivering several hundred horse-power and drove the line-shafting in all three spinning blocks. The octagonal chimney at the northern end of the whole complex, with its ironwork strapping, dates from 1853. The difference in scale between the 1813-18 wings and the 1845 wing is an indication of both the advances in mill architecture and steam-engine design, as well as the increasing size of the mule spinning machinery used in Manchester's mills which required larger and larger room widths.

Many of the new mills of the 1820s had direct access to the canal system. One of the best preserved 1820s mills is Brownsfield Mill (67). Built in 1825-26, the mill lies on the western side of Great Ancoats Street overlooking the Brownsfield lock on the Rochdale Canal and the eastern end of the Rochdale Canal basin. It was a steam-powered cotton spinning factory built as a room and power mill. The seven-storey southern wing was built around 1825 as a cotton spinning mill and had an internal engine house at the western gable. The northern six-storey wing was built shortly afterwards and by 1831 was in use as a warehouse and manufacturing block. It had a non-fireproof structure with wooden floors supported by heavy pine beams, many retaining their quality control marks showing they had been imported from the Baltic. Brownsfield Mill is notable for having the earliest surviving mill chimney-cum-stair house tower in Manchester, its highly unusual internal canal arm at the northern end of the northern wing and its covered courtyard. The power system remains are quite well preserved, with the engine house containing the original engine bed and evidence for two vertical drive shafts, one for each spinning block. The mill is of smaller proportions than some of the other surviving mills in the Ancoats area and at 6019m², with two wings of roughly 3000m² each, may be more representative of the Manchester cotton mill of the first third of the nineteenth century in its scale, with its six and seven storeys, its timber-floored construction and its canal-side location. A surviving parallel for this scale of building is Chatham Mill in Chorlton-on-Medlock.

Typical of the development of the power system in mills of the first half of the nineteenth century is the recently excavated engine house at Pin Mill on Pin Mill Brow (*68*). Established around 1794, possibly as a hand-powered or less likely a water-powered textile factory, shortly after 1800, a small Boulton and Watt type rotary engine was installed that would have produced 10 to 20hp. Only the brick plinth and some square-section iron bolts survived, its form may have been similar to the earliest steam engines in Manchester, such as that installed at Murray's Old Mill in 1798 (Williams with Farnie 1992). This was replaced by 1831 in Phase 2 with a larger beam engine, the remains for which are more fragmentary but include the site of a wagon boiler, flue and square-

67 Brownsfield Mill, built in the period 1825-6, had its own internal canal arm in the rear (left-hand) wing

68 The 1830s engine house at Pin Mill during demolition. Note the semi-circular flywheel recess behind the octagonal chimney

sectioned chimney. The output of this engine may have been around 100hp and it may have taken a form akin to contemporary steam engines built in Manchester by William Fairbairn and the engineering firm of Bateman and Sherratt, both based in Ancoats. This in turn was replaced in Phase 3, around 1849, by a much larger engine house, boiler house and chimney for a large beam engine of more than 100hp set on a tall stone and brick plinth that had later been converted to high pressure steam by the addition of a small high pressure cylinder. The context for this new engine house was the building of a large weaving shed on the western side of the mill complex. Such a rapid development sequence running from hand or water power through a small-scale steam engine and then a larger beamer engine appears to have been common in mills around Manchester in the first half of the nineteenth century.

By the mid nineteenth century most new cotton mills built within the city were fireproof and steam-powered structures with both spinning blocks and weaving sheds. These mill blocks could be found in the area between Oxford Road in the west and the Rochdale Canal basin in the east and were often served by short, private canal arms. Hanover Mill, demolished in 2000, was built a decade later than Brownsfield Mill in the 1830s and showed several technical developments in mill design. The main cotton spinning block was a large flat-roofed almost square structure of seven storeys and 10 by nine bays, with an internal engine house, a fireproof construction of brick vaulting and elevations featuring pilasters with stone cornices at each corner; it was surrounded by weaving sheds. Hanover Mill retained a number of notable features until its demolition, the most advanced being a fireproof floor construction using Hodgkinson's I-shaped cast iron beams; these had a wider bottom flange compared to the top flange and a parabolic profile. They were developed in the late 1820s in Manchester as a stronger, lighter form of fireproof construction and were used widely from 1831 (Fitzgerald 1988, 140; Williams with Farnie 1992, 80). In contrast, the staircase tower used flag-flooring supported by a complex grid of T-section cast iron beams, reminiscent of the fireproof floor construction at the nearby Beehive Mill in Ancoats, built in 1824 (Williams with Farnie 1992, 60-1).

The last major mill building boom in Manchester occurred during the years 1848 to 1853 (Williams with Farnie 1992, 21). The 1849-50 Ordnance Survey 60in to one mile map of Manchester records 172 textile mills and 91 textile finishing sites within the city, though it is unclear how many of these sites were functioning as mills. Nearly all of the mills were cotton spinning and weaving factories, although there was a silk finishing mill on Hardman Street. Mills could be found all over the centre of Manchester: on Long Millgate in the heart of the old medieval town and on Bridge Street in the Georgian town by the Irwell, though most were distributed along the Ashton and Rochdale Canals, beside private canal arms, and along the Rivers Irk, Irwell and Medlock. After 1850, new mills tended to be established in the suburbs around the city, although as early as 1825 mills were being built in Gorton and Newton on the eastern side of the city and at Beswick in 1828 (Williams with Farnie 1992, 21). This represented the peak of the industry in terms of manufacturing sites, though output did not reach its zenith, like the rest of the Lancashire cotton spinning industry, until 1913 at 3703 million working spindles (Williams with Farnie 1992, 46).

Mills from the 1840s and 1850s are a rarer survival in the city, but two notable structures are Doubling and Fireproof Mills on Bengal Street in Ancoats, both built around 1842 (64). The earliest is Doubling Mill, which as its name implies was used for doubling cotton, and retains its engine houses, circular stair tower and wooden floors supported by cast iron columns. Fireproof Mill, built in the period 1843-48, has a fireproof structure with brick barrel vaulting supported by Hodgkinson cast iron beams and columns, although the southern three bays were rebuilt in concrete. On the ground floor of this mill was a cart tunnel and three arched entrances indicating that this part of the mill was probably used for storage. These two brick mills were originally separate structures, but were linked in the 1880s when a new engine was installed and a new boiler house was built between the two structures.

Albert Mill, on the southern side of the Bridgewater Canal south-west of the Castlefield Canal basin, is one of a group of mid to late nineteenth-century textile mills built in the Hulme area. Begun in 1869, the mill is unusual because it is a rare survival of a textile smallware mill. It is one of the later mill complexes to survive within the city and belongs to a period when cotton spinning was in decline elsewhere in Manchester. The end products would then be sold to haberdashers, milliners and chapmen who carried and sold the products around the countryside. The smallwares were woven on special looms known as 'Dutch' looms or variously a ribbon loom, inkle loom or swivel loom. Several small shuttles were activated by the movement of a bar holding pegs that threw the shuttle across the loom by a swivelling action. This type of loom was able to weave a number of narrow fabrics simultaneously side by side and is thought to have originated in the Baltic Region in the late sixteenth century. By the eighteenth century, such looms were being used in Britain and smallware manufacture is attested in Manchester in the mid to late eighteenth century, but was not mechanised until the early nineteenth century.

The earliest phase at Albert Mill dates from 1869 and comprised a four-storey two-by-seven bay textile weaving mill, offices and boiler house with the stair tower at the southern end. In the period 1880 to 1890, the western end ground floor internal goods bay and associated warehouse flooring was built onto the first phase mill range with an external stair tower at the northern end. During 1895-1910, a three-storey northern range was built onto the western stair tower of the warehouse range. This building probably operated as a combined pattern and cutting floor with one or two of the storeys occupied with manual (treadle) sewing machines used for the manufacture of textile smallwares. Finally, around 1915 to 1920, the mill was extensively modernised with a single-storey, four bay machine floor built on the site of the northern mill yard. This expansion may have been due to production in the First World War and was associated with the use of electric sewing machines.

Of the late period mills in the city, three stand out, both metaphorically and literally. The tall chimney of Victoria Mill, in Miles Platting, can still be seen from Ancoats and remains a prominent landmark on the eastern side of the city (69). The mill was built in two phases in 1869 and 1873 as an architect-designed structure by George Woodhouse for the firm of William Holland (Hartwell, Hyde & Pevsner 2004, 382-3). It has a U-shaped plan formed by two large six-storey cotton spinning blocks linked by an engine house and a tall circular chimney that has a stair tower wrapped around the lower part. The overall appearance is Italianate, a popular design of the period, with red brick dressings and corner pilasters. The central engine house was replaced in 1902 with an external engine house for a horizontal steam engine that ran a rope drive in a rope race, a system which was introduced into Lancashire mills from the 1870s. Paragon and Royal Mill, both of six storeys and nine bays, were built in 1912 as additional wings to the McConnel and Kennedy's Ancoats complex and marked another major step in the development of the textile spinning industry, since both were built as electrically-powered mills, powered from Manchester's municipal grid. They were built of steel framing with concrete floors, hard flat roofs and drive-shaft towers for the electrically driven transmission system, and architectural ornamentation such as red brick with terracotta banding and Baroque detailing, typical of late period cotton spinning mills (Hartwell 2001, 280). However, they lack the monumentality of many Edwardian cotton spinning mills in Lancashire due to the small size of the urban plots they were built on. Paragon Mill used a plot of former workers' housing whilst Royal Mill was built on the site of McConnel and Kennedy's first 1798 mill.

The later history of Murray's Mills demonstrates the gradual decline of the Manchester cotton spinning industry in the later nineteenth century and early twentieth century.

69 Nineteenth-century mills along the Rochdale Canal. From left to right: Murray's, Doubling Mill and on the horizon Victoria Mill in Miles Platting

Production in the mid nineteenth century had stagnated so that in 1887 the company had 120,000 spindles and employed 500 people, roughly the same number of spindles, but fewer operatives than in the 1840s when Doubling and Fireproof mills were added to the complex (Miller & Wild 2007). Murray's Mills continued to be managed by family members until 1898 when they merged with 47 other Manchester cotton textile manufacturing firms, including such well known names as McConnel & Kennedy's and Houldsworths, to form the Fine Cotton Spinners and Doublers Association. Over the next 30 years this remained the largest and most successful cotton spinning manufacturing concern in the world, with over 60 mills (Williams with Farnie 1992, 20). The new company retained the Murray name and in 1910 A & G Murray Ltd was credited with 100,000 mule spindles and 20,000 doubling spindles. As late as 1930, Murray's Mills had 100,000 mule spindles and 30,000 doubling spindles. The collapse of the Lancashire cotton industry in the 1930s led to a sharp decline in the number of Manchester mills operating and in 1948 and 1950 the Fine Cotton Spinners and Doublers Ltd conveyed the whole of the complex to two or more separate companies. It was probably in this period that large-scale cotton production ceased on most sites.

The number of working cotton mills in Manchester reached around 1850 and thereafter declined, with the city being surpassed as the chief centre of the cotton spinning industry by Bolton in the 1850s and by Oldham in the 1860s (Williams with Farnie 1992, 21). The decline in cotton manufacturing accelerated after 1883 and only a handful of mills were built in the city in the late nineteenth century; these were mainly in the Miles Platting district east of Ancoats, for example Manchester's last cotton spinning mill built in 1924 for W.H. Holland & Sons Ltd.

In the early twenty-first century it is possible to stand on the towpath of the Rochdale Canal next to Murray's Mills and look eastwards across Ancoats and Miles Platting at a line of textile mills that span nearly all the main developments of the city's factory-based cotton spinning industry; from the first steam-powered factories of the 1790s such as Murray's, through the arrival of fireproofing as at Doubling Mill, to the suburban mills such as Victoria, and to the final phase of electrically driven mills of the 1910s and 1920s, represented by Paragon Mill. This vista remains a revolutionary scene.

MANCHESTER'S SECOND TRANSPORT REVOLUTION

The development of transport infrastructure in and around Manchester during the late eighteenth and nineteenth centuries both fed and was fed by the town's growing trade and textile manufacturing base.

The extension of the canal network was a key factor in the industrial development of the eastern side of the city around Piccadilly and Ancoats from the 1790s to the 1830s. The first canal in this area was the Ashton, which was authorised by an Act of Parliament in 1792. Its purpose was to carry coal to Manchester from the collieries of the Ashton and Oldham areas. Green's Map of 1794 indicates its proposed line through the southern side of Ancoats. In the 1820s this corridor was dominated by a line of multi-storey, steam-powered cotton spinning mills. The canal opened between Ashton and Ancoats in 1796 (Hadfield & Biddle 1970, 294-5). Crossing Store Street is a skewed canal aqueduct, designed by the canal engineer Benjamin Outram, which is the earliest surviving example of its kind in the country. The Rochdale Canal received its Act in 1794 and was built to provide a trans-Pennine route between Yorkshire and south-east Lancashire by connecting with the Calder and Hebble Navigation at Sowerby Bridge. In 1800 the first element to be completed of the westernmost section of the canal was the stretch between Castlefield (70) and the Rochdale Canal basin (71) off Dale Street, linking the south-western and south-eastern sides of the city by water. Ancoats itself was not served by the canal until 1804 when the system was completed. By this date several textile mill complexes, such as McConnel and Kennedy's and Murray's, had been built along its northern side. In the early nineteenth century, further ribbon industrial development along the Rochdale spread eastwards towards Newton Heath. Both canals facilitated the transport of raw materials, finished goods and the coal vital to Manchester's cotton mills.

A significant feature of the Ashton and Rochdale Canals through Manchester was the side branches or short private canal arms (72). The first of these canal arms was the short stretch serving the Grocer's Warehouse that was in use by 1770 (Nevell 2003, 45). By 1794 four such canal arms ran off the Castlefield canal basin; three to serve canal warehouses

70 Much of the surviving fabric of the Castlefield Canal Basin, such as the Merchant's Warehouse here, dates from the early nineteenth-century expansion of the system

and a transhipment shed and one serving a lime works. The longest of these was 150m. By 1850 there were 33 canal arms east of the Castlefield Canal basin, the longest of which ran off the Ashton Canal in Ancoats, under Pollard Street, and was around 410m.

Probably the first canal arm along the Rochdale Canal was a 183m arm running north of the canal on the eastern side of Oxford Road. This was opened by 1800 to serve Pickford's Warehouse on Dickinson Street. Around the same time two substantial canal arms were built on the northern side of the Ashton Canal in Ancoats. Each was more than 185m and ran either side of the modern Vesta Street. One of the more extraordinary canal arms in Manchester was the tunnelled stretch leading off the north side of the Rochdale Canal in Ancoats underneath Union Street to the canal basin in the courtyard at Murray's Mill. This was opened around 1805, shortly after the Rochdale Canal was extended through Ancoats.

71 The interior of the Rochdale Warehouse on Dale Street built by the Rochdale Canal Company in 1806 at their Piccadilly basin. The floors were supported by cast iron columns with slots to create storage partitions

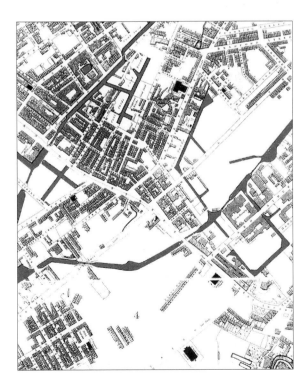

72 The expansion of the canal system in the city during the early nineteenth century was led by the building of private canal arms which by 1831 totalled more than three miles in length. The most extensive network was in Ancoats, as seen here on Bank's map of Manchester from 1831

By 1808 there were six canal arms in Castlefield running off the Bridgewater Canal, seven running off the Ashton Canal and 12 branches from the Rochdale, amounting to almost 3km of extra canal. In 1831 there were six such branches in Castlefield, eight canal arms along the Ashton Canal and 17 branching from the Rochdale Canal, with a total length of around 5.25km. By 1848-50 this had risen to 11 branches off the Bridgewater Canal in Castlefield (most of the new ones serving a line of mid nineteenth-century cotton spinning mills to the south-west of the basin along the southern side of the Bridgewater), 13 branches along the Ashton (including a series of short arms between Great Ancoats Streets and the Ashton Canal basin that serviced cotton mills, ironworks and warehouses) and 20 off the Rochdale Canal, running to around 5.6km. More than half of this network had been built by 1808 and 80 per cent by 1831. However, there were significant additions made between 1831 and 1850, an era usually seen as dominated by the coming of the railways. These included two stretches, each more than 180m, running south of the Rochdale Canal, to the west and east of Sackville Street, crossing the line of Shooters Brook. The canal arm running northwards off the Rochdale behind Chepstow Street became the eastern end of the Manchester and Salford Junction Canal, which linked the Rochdale Canal with the eastern bank of the River Irwell on Quay Street. At the western end of the canal close to Lock No. 2 and the tunnel entrance was the 97m long Brunswick Wharf. There were even some late nineteenth-century additions to this network, such as the short arm built off the southern side of the Bridgewater Canal south-west of the Castlefield Canal basin to service the new Hulme Corn Mills.

Few of these canal arms, or the main canals, have been excavated, largely because most of these canal arms have been filled and buried, and also due to the fact that the main routes of the Ashton, Bridgewater and Rochdale Canals remain in use, though now principally travelled by pleasure craft. The canal basin and tunnel at Murray's Mills is one such site that has been excavated, but perhaps more typical are the canal arms off Pot Street and at the end of Newton Street (opposite Murray's Mill and running off the southern side of the Rochdale Canal). Excavations across both these features showed them to be of typical canal construction with a puddled clay floor and brick side walls capped with stone blocks to form the edge of the tow path. Few of these private canal arms survive. The one running northwards off the Rochdale Canal behind Chepstow Street survives in part and now comes out just behind the Bridgewater Concert Hall, instead of Hall Street further to the east. The branch running north-westwards under Mosley Street has also been excavated, as has Hulme Lock, which provided access between the Bridgewater Canal and the Mersey and Irwell Navigation in Castlefield (73).

There is one major canal that has been investigated archaeologically because most of its line is now abandoned – the Manchester and Salford Junction that was built in the years 1836-39 (74). Locks No. 1 and 2 of the Manchester Salford Junction Canal were rediscovered and excavated in 1989 when the Granada Television Company had an area of subsidence in their main car park, to the west of Water Street and adjacent to the Television Centre. The canal had been backfilled with loose rubble, whilst the lower 2m of this fill was bedded in a matrix of oily, organic silt that would have accumulated in the lock when the canal was nearing the end of its active life. The southern pound of the pair of locks that formed Lock No. 2 had survived virtually intact and was defined by two parallel brick walls, their faces 4.7m apart and 5.65m deep. These are capped by an overhanging stone coping, originally defining the towpath edges. A thick stone string course, *c.*2m below the coping, defined the upper water level when the locks were active, while the lower water level is defined by a second course, some 4.2m below coping level. The wall footing was carried on a fourth stone course, from which the brick arched invert of the canal bed sprang. The brickwork in the walls consisted of regular coursing in English bond, with alternate courses of headers effectively tying in the face of the wall to the back.

Immediately west of the Lock No. 2 is the still intact Irwell Bridge carrying Water Street over the Manchester and Salford Junction Canal. West of that are the remains of Lock No. 1, which controlled access to and from the River Irwell. One surprising result revealed by the excavations was the level of water in Lock No. 1 when compared to Lock No. 2. Lock No. 1 should have been constructed to accommodate both flood and drought conditions on the River Irwell and so allow traffic to enter or leave the canal at

73 Albert Mill, a rare smallware mill from 1869, lies on the southern side of the Bridgewater Canal south-west of Castlefield. It is one of a group of later nineteenth-century textile mills built in the Hulme area beside several short canal arms

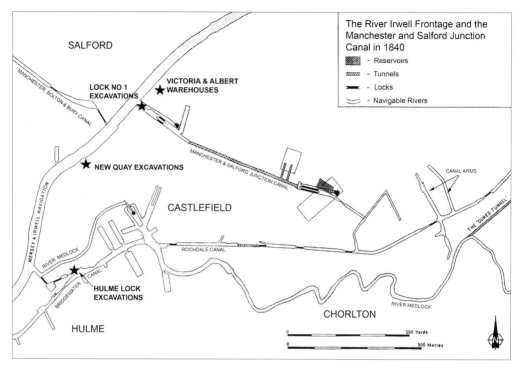

74 A plan of the Irwell River frontage and the Manchester and Salford Junction Canal in 1840

all times. The mean water level of the Irwell was determined as *c*.21.8m above sea level in 1989. If this level is projected into the canal terminus, Lock No. 1 would appear to have been rendered obsolete – that is traffic could have moved through the pound without the lock gates being applied all year round. Possibly Lock No. 1 was constructed to be used in extreme drought conditions but it seems more likely that the River Irwell's channel became severely silted up after the lock was built, raising the river level by more than a metre. There is documentary evidence to show that the river bed of the Irwell along Water Street had been raised by the dumping of thousands of tons of cinders during the late nineteenth century. Whatever the explanation for this anomaly, the practical result was that in the second half of the nineteenth century, a boat would have been able to run from the river directly into Lock No. 2, passing through Lock No. 1 without stopping in all but drought conditions, speeding the flow of goods along the canal. The irony is that had the redundant Lock No. 1 not been built, it could have the reduced the cost of the canal's construction as well as speeding up traffic flow, thus improving the route's competitiveness with the rival, and more successful, Hulme Lock scheme on the Bridgewater Canal (Nevell 2004).

Whilst the canal network continued to expand within the city during the first few decades of the nineteenth century, so did river traffic on the Irwell (Nevell 2004). The tonnage figures for the trade carried by the Mersey and Irwell Navigation before 1816 are very difficult to establish due to a lack of documentary evidence, in contrast to the extensive material that survives for the Bridgewater Canal. Nevertheless, what is available indicates that most of this trade was carried by the Navigation company's own crafts and was dominated by bulk cargos. In 1816 this amounted to, according to Hadfield and Biddle, roughly 93,000 tons, which grew to *c.*123,000 tons in 1820 and *c.*133,000 in 1823; the figure was even higher by 1830, though by how much is unclear (Hadfield & Biddle 116-7). Independent carriers added roughly an extra 10 per cent to these figures (Hadfield & Biddle 1970, 102). There were new opportunities being developed in these two decades. The year 1807 saw the opening of a passenger boat service along the Navigation, the first direct competition with the Bridgewater Canal. The Manchester, Bolton and Bury Canal, opened in 1808, was designed to provide a link for the textile mills and collieries north-west of Manchester with the Navigation at Salford Old Quay, and boost the flow of trade along the Irwell. In 1813 a market boat service carrying food produce from northern Cheshire began, again in direct competition with the Bridgewater Canal. This growth and diversification in trade is a reflection of the rapid industrial and commercial growth of Manchester during this period.

From studying the early maps of the area it can be seen that major development of the Water Street river frontage did not begin until the late eighteenth century. Yate's map of 1786 shows no evidence of large-scale activity around the Irwell-Medlock confluence, but Laurent's map of 1793 clearly shows the burgeoning industrial growth of this area. Although much of the trade along the Mersey and Irwell was carried by the boats of the Navigation, it did not have a monopoly, especially as trade increased in the early nineteenth century. In 1822, the New Quay Company was established on a site at the southern end of Water Street (75). The site was the subject of excavation by GMAU in the early 1990s and remains the only section of the Irwell waterfront so far investigated in the city (Hadfield & Biddle 1970, 101-2). The New Quay Company was set up by John Brettargh and two partners with an initial capital of £30,000. Carrying mainly shop goods to and from Liverpool, the company enjoyed commercial success, owning 18 craft by 1825 and eventually operating 25. Banck's map of 1831 shows the complex as a linear arrangement of buildings running south-east from the river bank, with a U-shaped arrangement of stables along the Water Street frontage. After the establishment of this second wharf area, the original quay site became commonly referred to as the Old Quay Company (Nevell 2004).

In 1990-91 seven trenches were opened by machine and were excavated directly onto natural sands and gravels. Archaeological deposits were located in three trenches, A, B and C, running west to east at 90 degrees from the present course of the River Irwell. The most significant of these remains were those of an early nineteenth-century timber waterfront in Trench A (Nevell 2004). This waterfront, set some 12m east of the modern river embankment, consisted of timber revetting forming a roughly semi-circular berth and represented the north-eastern rim of the New Quay basin as shown on Banck's map of 1831. The basin and its associated features were cut into an area of riverine deposits lying in a hollow or inlet in the natural gravel river terrace. These deposits contained no finds or evidence of human activity and appeared to be part of the Irwell floodplain. The waterfront itself was sealed by a series of dumps of Victorian

75 Excavations on the site of Lock No. 1 on the Manchester and Salford Junction Canal in 1989 revealed the well-preserved stone and timber lock structure

household waste, showing that it fell out of use in the late nineteenth century, making way for the present riverfront. Set roughly 6 to 7m behind the timbers of the exposed revetments were a series of east to west running slots interpreted as robbed out beam slots and possibly representing a timber wharf or jetty construction. If this is the case, then they were earlier than the revetment to the west and fell out of use with the silting up of the inlet, probably representing the primary phase of the New Quay structures on this site.

A group of brick-built structures were located towards the northern limit of Trench A. These features can be readily linked to cartographic evidence, helping to provide a more comprehensive depiction of the nineteenth-century topography of the area. In the north-eastern corner of the trench, lying some 9m behind the revetment, a 7m length of wall was revealed. Running east-west, it is well constructed and survived to a maximum height of three courses. Three brick buttresses were incorporated into the wall's southern face and a north-running return at its western end indicates that it formed the southern side of a building. This building is almost certainly that shown as the northernmost building of the New Quay Company's yards on maps from 1831 onwards. Abutting the wall and the buttresses was a 7m by 4.5m area of poorly laid brickwork, forming an external floor or yard surface. Composed almost entirely from broken and re-used bricks and with a kerbed edge forming its southern limit, it had been extensively damaged by later truncation.

These excavations demonstrate the potential for the survival of late eighteenth- and nineteenth-century waterside remains along the eastern bank of the River Irwell through the city centre.

The other major surviving element of the Irwell waterfront is the Victoria and Albert Warehouse complex to the north of the New Quay site. The western L-shaped structure, the Victoria Warehouse, was built in 1838-40, with the eastern building – the six bay Albert Warehouse – being added after 1849, and involved the filling in of an earlier quay. These buildings presently cover a floor area of 7547m², but this was a two phase complex and the original L-shaped western warehouse was only 5489m² in area, making it slightly smaller that the Bridgewater's Middle Warehouse, completed in 1831, with a floor area of 6175m².

The complex now forms a five storey, brick-built, slate-roofed, L-shaped structure, built on sandstone foundations. Externally the buildings are very imposing. The northern river frontage is 58.5m wide, 20 bays long, with four loading bays facing the river. There is a two-bay-wide, two-storey arched cart entrance defined by ashlar blocks five bays from the eastern gable. The western canal frontage is 48m and 15 bays long, but with just one loading bay. The eastern three bays of this elevation do not contain any windows because originally there was another multi-storey building running at right angles to the warehouse along Water Street. The southern courtyard frontage is 12 bays and 32m long with three loading bays and another two-bay-wide, two-storey arched cart entrance defined by rusticated ashlar blocks, one bay from the western edge of the courtyard. The Water Street frontage is only 16.8m or five bays long. It is set at a slight angle to incorporate the earlier line of the street and has a central one-bay-wide, two-storey arched cart entrance, again defined by ashlar blocks.

There are a few clues externally that show that the Albert Warehouse is later. These are the brick parapet that at roof level can be seen to divide the two structures, the roof line of the Albert Warehouse, which is slightly higher than hipped roof of the Victoria Warehouse, and the style of the loading bays which have brick arches with a stone keystone just below the roof level, as opposed to the square-headed loading bays in the Victoria Warehouse. Both have low six-pane tilting casement windows, with raised stone sills and flat-arched heads. Internally, the differences between the two structures are greater. The Victoria Warehouse was built with wooden floors supported by large transverse pine timbers that were in turn supported by slotted iron columns giving a series of large open L-shaped floor spaces. Many of the cast iron columns had four vertical paired flanges to allow the introduction of wooden partitions for separating different goods. Access to the upper storeys was via a staircase at the inner angle of the complex opposite the courtyard. The roof structure comprised a series of large strutted king post trusses supporting a hipped roof. The Albert Warehouse also had thick wooden floors supported by pine timbers and cast iron columns, but here the timbers were arranged longitudinally and there was a central cross wall, perhaps as a fireproofing feature. Access was via its own staircase in the south-eastern corner of the building.

The hoist system in both warehouses was manually driven with cast iron flywheels in the loft powered by ropes that dropped through holes in all five floors, some adjacent to large trapdoors so that they could be used internally. The loading openings throughout the complex had cathead cranes and there was direct loading from boats on the riverside where the warehouses were built flush with the river bank.

The Victoria and Albert Warehouses is now the only such complex to survive along the River Irwell and they were converted in 1991-92 into hotel accommodation, though the name continues. This complex remains the most visible monument to the Navigation Company and when combined with the later transhipment shed that abuts the eastern end of the complex, the whole forms the longest continuous nineteenth-century waterfront to survive within the city, at roughly 135m long.

Whilst the canal system and the Irwell river frontage remain impressive landscapes, the greatest transport innovation within the nineteenth-century city was the development of the railway network. Visitors to the Castlefield area cannot help but notice how the canal network is overshadowed by six brick and cast iron railway viaducts that criss-cross the area, perhaps the most visible demonstration of the rise and success of the railways (76). The Victorian city was served by four mainline terminal stations (Central, Liverpool Road, Piccadilly and Victoria), two intermediate stations (Deansgate and Oxford Road) and two major goods depots (the Great Northern Railway warehouse complex and the Oldham Road depot). Like many of the great industrial towns of the nineteenth century,

76 The Castlefield Canal basin was the most important transport terminus in Manchester until the opening of the Liverpool to Manchester railway in 1830

77 The façade of Liverpool Road station, the first intercity passenger station in the world, looks more like a Georgian townhouse than a railway station, largely because no one knew what a railway station should look like

the railway stations ring the city centre, which was already cluttered with factories, houses, shops and warehouses by the time Liverpool Road was opened in 1830. Most of this railway infrastructure still survives with the exception of Oldham Street and parts of the Great Northern site.

The best known railway site is Liverpool Road Station and this is justly famous as the eastern terminus of the world's first intercity passenger railway; it has the first intercity passenger station and the oldest surviving railway warehouse (*77*). From its inception in 1821, and then the opening of the line in September 1830, the railway was viewed as a momentous achievement in transport history (Fitzgerald 1980; Greene 1995). The choice of the Liverpool Road terminus was in part dictated by access to the west and thus Liverpool, the need to clear the River Irwell at a sufficient height to allow Navigation boats through and in part by the availability of suitable land that landowners were willing to sell to the railway company. The site was something of a compromise. It required bridging the line across the Irwell floodplain and taking the track onto the top of the sandstone bluff that formed Castlefield. These topographical problems are in part responsible for the form of the buildings on the site. The two-storey passenger station fronts the northern side of Liverpool Road and is terraced into the western side of the hill. It has a domestic-looking, classical façade faced in stone and stucco, and the first and second class booking offices are on the ground floor. Access to the track was at first floor level on the northern side of the building, via separate staircases, where passengers climbed aboard the carriages using steps (Hartwell 2001, 266; Parkinson-Bailey 2000, 49). The lack of raised platform with an overhead canopy – features typical of railway stations later in the century – indicate that this was an experimental building; after all no one knew what a passenger railway station should look like.

The adjacent 1830 railway warehouse, erected in just five months, was an unusual structure that appears to have drawn on canal transhipment traditions (Greene 1995; McNeil 2004) (*78*). Initially the Liverpool and Manchester Railway Company had tried to negotiate warehouse facilities with the New Quay Company on neighbouring Water Street. When that failed, the company built their own warehouse. This was almost certainly designed by Thomas Haigh, the Liverpool architect. Haigh appears to have adapted a design originally turned down for the Gloucester docks. The three-storey building, which bends to meet the curve of the railway line and had six spur tracks running into the southern side of the building, bears more than a passing resemblance to the classic style of canal warehouse with its split levels and internal loading bays (Hartwell 2001, 267; Taylor, Cooper & Barnwell 2002, 17). Internally, the structure was timber-framed with long softwood tie-beams that had Baltic marks stamped on them (*79*). There was also a series of cross-walls dividing the interior into separate storage units, just as in the late eighteenth-century extension to the Grocer's Warehouse in Castlefield. The original gravity-assisted hoist system was soon found to be inadequate due to the heavy usage of the warehouse, so in 1831 a steam-powered system was introduced. The base of this beam engine at the western end of the warehouse was excavated in 1992; it indicates that it was a substantial beam engine perhaps capable of producing more than 50hp. The Liverpool Road railway complex, which now forms part of the Museum of Science and Industry, later expanded to include a transfer shed built in 1855, the 1865 Bonded Goods Warehouse and, in 1880, a large four-storey warehouse on Lower Byrom Street.

By 1849 two further terminal stations had opened in Manchester. London Road, or Piccadilly as it was later known, opened in 1842. It was run jointly by the Manchester and Birmingham Railway and the Sheffield, Ashton-under-Lyne and Manchester Railway. The elaborate wrought iron roof, which is the earliest element of the structure to survive and still dominates the platform side of the station, dates from 1880-83. Hunts Bank, later Victoria station, opened in 1844 and was run by the Liverpool and Manchester Railway. It was initially designed by Robert Stephenson, but was extended in the 1880s and 1903, the latter producing the long and impressive Baroque façade which can be seen today (Hartwell 2001, 215-7, 237-8). In the 1840s the commercial importance of Manchester led to nine railway companies competing for access to the city, more than any other urban centre outside London. By 1860, amalgamation and commercial sense had reduced these to three companies; the London and North Western worked out of Piccadilly, as did the Manchester, Sheffield and Lincolnshire, and the Lancashire and Yorkshire Railway were the sole users of Victoria Station (Kidd 2002, 113). Liverpool Road closed to passenger traffic in 1855, although it remained a goods station until the 1970s.

78 The 1830 Railway Warehouse (centre), now part of the Museum of Science and Industry, received its goods at first floor level and unloaded the railway trucks inside the building, just like a classic canal warehouse

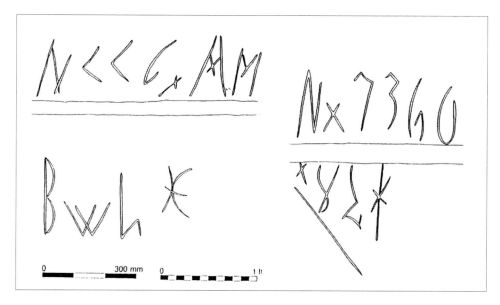

79 Baltic timber marks from the 1830 Warehouse. These quality control marks can be found in many of Manchester's late eighteenth- and nineteenth-century industrial buildings, highlighting the trade in softwoods with the Baltic (*image courtesy of GMAU*)

In the 1880s and 1890s, two major additions to the railway network in the city substantially changed the urban landscape of Manchester (*80*). Central Station, now the Manchester Exhibition Centre, was the last station to be opened in the city centre, in 1880, and has a wrought iron segmental vaulted roof with a span of 210ft (64m) that is 90ft (29.5m) high at its apex. It was inspired by St Pancras in London, opened 12 years earlier in 1868, which also had a wrought iron segmental vaulted roof with a larger span of 74m and a height of 32m, making it overall 15 per cent bigger than Central Station. Beneath

80 The railway viaducts of the Castlefield area, looking east (*Copyright GMAU/English Heritage*)

81 The Great Northern Railway's Goods Warehouse, built in the 1890s, was a huge complex covering more than 20,000m² and was the last major addition to the city centre's railway network

this huge wrought iron arch was a vast brick undercroft with intersecting tunnel vaults that was used for storage and had wagon lifts from the adjacent goods sidings (Hartwell 2001, 209). Today this is a car park. Between 1895 and 1898 the Great Northern Railway Company built an extensive warehouse complex on the eastern side of Deansgate and immediately west of Central Station (*81*). It provided road, rail and canal interchange in a five-storey warehouse built over the line of the Manchester & Salford Junction Canal. The external elevations of the warehouse are in the Italianate style whilst the internal structure is notable for the early use of steel pillars and lengthwise and crosswise riveted steel beams that supported brick arches. The lowest two levels contained rails and turntables on each floor connected to each other by inclines with hydraulic haulage. Whilst this structure survives, having been converted into a car park and entertainment centre, the two-storey marshalling yards to south, along with massive brick approach viaduct that spanned Deansgate itself were demolished in the early years of the twenty-first century.

Even with the addition of Central Station, the northern and southern sides of the city centre remained without a direct rail connection, a gap in the city's transport network that was not filled until the building of the Metrolink system in the early 1990s.

Of equal significance with these four terminal city centre stations was the opening in 1849 of the Manchester South Junction and Altrincham Railway, whose brick railway viaduct of 224 arches still carries the line from Piccadilly in the east, across Oxford Road and the site of the Roman fort in Castlefield, to Liverpool Road in the west. The key to understanding the significance of this monument, though, lies in the shorter branch viaduct running south-west towards Cornbrook and the line to Altrincham. This line is notable as being probably Britain's first dedicated suburban passenger railway line and marks the beginning of the extension of the city's influence southwards towards the market towns of Stretford and Altrincham. Within a few years, dormitory villages, with semi-detached and detached villa-style residences for the Manchester middle classes, had sprung up around the intermediate stations of Sale and Timperley, and the fringes of the two market towns saw the building of villa residences (Nevell 1997, 97-101). Of the early stations, only that at Old Trafford, which has a classically-designed booking hall, built around 1856, now survives.

Elsewhere within the city, north Manchester was served by the Lancashire and Yorkshire Railway from 1849 when the line to Middleton and Rochdale opened, with stations at Newton Heath and Moston (Rush 1983, 4-5). The Stockport, Timperley and Altrincham Junction Railway, opened in 1866, serviced Northenden in the southern part of the city, whilst a line from the Cornbrook East Junction to Glazebrook, and then Cressington Junction near Liverpool, opened in 1873, giving access to the villages of Urmston and Flixton south-west of Manchester, which were soon to become new dormitory towns for the city (Griffiths 1958, 52-3; Hodgkins 2004, 121-8). Other suburban lines were opened through Burnage, Withington and Didsbury to the south of the city in 1880, and to Belle Vue and Gorton to the east by 1885 (Kidd 2002, 113, 146; Rose 1987, 6).

During the mid to late nineteenth century, suburban railway lines were important for several reasons: they allow the middle classes to leave the by now heavily industrialised city for more rural areas and also paved the way for the growth of suburban communities dependent upon Manchester, facilitating the expansion of the city's boundaries to the south and east.

WAREHOUSE CITY

Manchester's dominance as a commercial and financial centre in the second half of the nineteenth century was dependent in part on its success as a textile manufacturing and marketing town and its role as the most important transport hub in the region. The physical expression of its commercial and financial role was the large number of warehouses built within the city centre. These warehouses were notable for two reasons: the way in which they came to dominate various parts of the city and the development of the goods handling and marketing process.

In the late eighteenth century there were very few dedicated warehouses within Manchester, the city's first trade directory recording 38 warehouses within the town in 1772 (Nevell 2003, 35). Later eighteenth-century trade directories indicate that warehouse facilities were concentrated around Shambles Square and the western, Deansgate, end of Market Street and many were associated with coaching inns and public houses (Nevell 2003, 35-6).

The earliest purpose-built warehouses to survive within the city are those associated with the canal network around the Castlefield Canal basin on the Bridgewater Canal and later the Ashton and Rochdale Canal basins. Although the first canal warehouses built in the city were the Grocers' and Duke's Warehouses, the most complete of these early warehouses was the Rochdale Canal Warehouse on Dale Street, which has survived

82 The Dale Street (Rochdale) Warehouse is the only stone warehouse building in the city

almost intact from 1806 (*82*). It is distinguished by the use of stone in the structure rather than brick and the use of cast iron columns to support the timber beams and wooden floors. The two shipping holes for the internal canal arms can still be seen in its eastern elevation and the flywheels for the hoist system have recently been incorporated within the attic space of the renovated structure. What is not apparent is the cast iron waterwheel installed in 1824, which ran the hoist system and which still survives in a wheelpit buried beneath southern end of the warehouse. Elsewhere, in Castlefield, are two huge and rather fine canal warehouses, the Merchant's Warehouse of 1825 and the Middle Warehouse from 1831, whilst the latest canal warehouse to survive in the city is the 1836 Tariff Street Warehouse on the northern side of the Rochdale basin (Nevell 2003, 36-7). This is five storeys high and has a single arched shipping hole in the southern elevation and brick cross-walls. The hoist system, unlike that at Dale Street, but like those at the Merchant's and Middle Warehouses, appears to have been hand-powered throughout the nineteenth century, though in the early twentieth century it was converted to hydraulic and then electric power.

The opening in September 1830 of the Liverpool Road terminus of the Liverpool and Manchester Railway marks the rise of the railway system as the most important long-distance transport network in the region during the nineteenth century. The Liverpool Road Warehouse is the earliest surviving urban railway warehouse in Britain, though it is a transitional structure with many affinities to the earlier canal warehouse tradition (Greene 1995, 1). The introduction of cast iron framing in the 1850s and subsequently wrought iron followed by steel framing, enabled railway companies to build larger and higher warehouses than those next to the canals. In the second half of the nineteenth century, Manchester's railway termini attracted multi-storey square-plan warehouses with iron, and later steel, framing. The London Road railway warehouse was opened in 1867, behind Piccadilly Station, and showcases many of these new features (*83*). A bonded warehouse, it is a nearly square structure with seven storeys all in brick. There was railway access on the ground floor from the north-eastern side via four sets of tracks and road access from the south-west side. Internally, the fireproof structure used an innovative technique to exploit the tensile strength of wrought iron and thereby achieve greater spans. The 0.65m-wide cast iron columns, which supported wrought iron box girders that carried intermediate cast iron beams for brick arches, diminished in circumference

83 The London Road railway warehouse, opened in the 1860s

on each floor. The 1869 bonded warehouse on the northern side of Liverpool Road also displays these features, although it has cruciform columns, as does the adjacent 1880 Lower Byrom Street Warehouse, which was served by a viaduct supported by thick cast iron columns. This is now the main exhibition area for the Museum of Science and Industry (Hartwell 2001, 268). These design changes culminated with the building of the Great Northern Railway warehouse in the years 1895-98. This is a five-storey multi-purpose canal, rail and road interchange with a floor area of more than 26,700m² and a first floor level railway connection. It encompassed state of the art construction technology, in the form of one of the first large steel-framed buildings in Britain, with steel stanchions supporting longitudinally-riveted wrought iron girders and brick-arched fireproof floors.

By 1850 Manchester's warehouses (canal, rail and commercial) were concentrated in three distinct areas – along the eastern bank of the River Irwell along Water Street, around the Castlefield Canal basin, and around the Ashton and Rochdale Canal Basins off Ducie Street.

Despite the national importance of the canal and railway warehouse structures, it was the commercial warehouse that came to typify Manchester's role as a warehouse centre and large parts of the city centre remain dominated by dozens of these buildings (Taylor, Cooper & Barnwell 2002). Typically they serviced the textile industry and emerged in large numbers from the 1840s, with examples being built as late as the 1920s, in an area running from Oxford Street in the west to London Road in the east. Friedrich Engels writing in 1842-43 noted that the city had already developed

> a rather extended commercial district, perhaps about half a mile long and about as broad, and consisting almost wholly of offices and warehouses. Nearly the whole district is abandoned by dwellers, and is lonely and deserted at night …
>
> Bradshaw 1987, 38

So emblematic did these commercial warehouses become of the city's commercial and industrial prowess, with their multiple roles as advertising symbol, statement of industrial power and prestige, and practical storage facility, that they became simply known as the Manchester Warehouses (Cooper 1991).

What is usually regarded as the first Manchester Warehouse was the five-storey, brick-built, wooden-floored cast iron-column-supported 14-16 Mosley Street, erected in 1839. Designed by one of the city's most notable architect's, Edward Walters, for Richard Cobden, it used the Italian palazzo style for the main elevation, inspired by fourteenth- and fifteenth-century architecture of the great Italian merchant cities of Florence, Genoa, and Venice, and became the dominant architectural style of the Manchester Warehouse until the end of the century. Its layout also set the template for the way in which the Manchester Warehouse functioned. This building thus marked the emergence of the commercial warehouse as a showplace, wholesale shop and office, providing a powerful link between the local textile industry and the international market for British textiles. Most of these warehouses, though, were run by companies separate from the mill owners, so that once an order was placed, the warehouse buyer would order grey cloth from the cotton mill, have it finished in a bleaching, dyeing and print works, and then packaged and shipped to the client, thus developing a large dedicated wholesale sector within the city. Such was the dominance of Manchester and its merchants of the wholesale and commercial side of the cotton industry that in the second half of the nineteenth century cotton goods throughout the world became known simply as 'Manchester Goods'.

These warehouses, which could be as large as a cotton spinning mill complex, were divided into three main types: home trade warehouses, multiple occupancy warehouses and overseas warehouses. Home trade warehouses, which can be found all over the warehouse district but with large numbers around Charlotte Street, Dale Street, and Portland Street, were the most elaborately decorated (Hartwell, Hyde & Pevsner 2004, 310-1, 326-8). Each floor was divided into departments that specialised in particular types of goods overseen by a foreman who supervised assistants and salesmen. The lightest goods were stored on the upper floors and the heavier goods on the lowest floors. These sales floors were used as sample and pattern rooms with benches for cloth examination which required plenty of light, hence the many windows. In the basement of the warehouse was the packing floor with boilers, presses, later on hydraulic gear and other services such as inspection and making-up; orders were lowered to the packing floor via hoists. Opposite the main entrance was a grand staircase that penetrated the full height of the building to impress prospective buyers, and led to the ground floor, where the company's offices were located along with entertainment rooms and showrooms for the clients (Cooper 1991; Taylor, Cooper & Barnwell 2002, 21). Amongst the many fine mid nineteenth-century surviving examples within the city are 36 Charlotte Street, a palazzo-style warehouse designed by Edward Walters and built in 1855-60, and S & J Watt's huge warehouse on Portland Street, now the Britannia Hotel, built in 1855-58, which uses a different architectural style on each floor (*84*).

Multiple occupancy warehouses, a feature of Manchester's commercial quarter since the early nineteenth century, continued to be popular. Such structures were owned by a company that provided storage, display, office and packing space which was rented to a number of smaller companies, rather on the lines of the room and power mills of the early nineteenth century. Such buildings were used by companies involved in both the home and overseas market. One of the finest surviving examples is Canada House on Chepstow Street (*85*). Built in 1909, this is a six storey, ten bay structure with wide windows within a terracotta façade, whilst the rear elevation is a glazed screen with octagonal piers rising the full height of the building. Inside, every floor had its own offices reached by a grand central staircase (Hartwell, Hyde & Pevsner 2004, 310-1).

Export warehouses, often owned by German and Greek shippers, are mostly clustered along Princess Street and Whitworth Street, and followed the same layout as the home trade warehouses, though showrooms were less common. Architecturally these buildings tended to be plainer, though there was still a clear division between the elaborate main face and the functional rear with its multiple loading bays, often to be found backing onto a canal (Taylor, Cooper & Barnwell 2002, 23). Amongst the finest surviving examples within the city are Asia House, Central House, India House and Lancaster House, all along Princess Street. These late period steel-framed structures built between 1890 and 1914 marked the pinnacle of this type of warehouse and included the hydraulic hoist systems run from the city's newly installed hydraulic supply. The use of steel-framing allowed for larger structures and freer use of more architectural styles, from Classical and Italianate, Elizabethan and Scottish, to Renaissance and French Baroque.

This is perhaps best exemplified by two buildings on Oxford Street, which whilst not being strictly Manchester Warehouses, nevertheless owed their existence and monumentality to this building type. The Refuge Assurance Company building, now the Palace Hotel and still retaining its iconic clock tower, was built in three phases between 1891 and 1932, using the architects Alfred Waterhouse, Paul Waterhouse and Stanley Birkett. The main façades use Italianate designs in dark red terracotta, whilst the rear elevations are in glazed white brick and are equally startling. Inside, the ground floor was one single, open business hall, whilst each building had its own elegant staircase (Parkinson-Bailey 2000, 132-3). St James' Buildings were built in 1912-13 for the Calico Printers Association, a grouping of more than 50 finishing firms, and were designed as the company's offices,

84 Watts' Warehouse, now the Britannia Hotel, is the most flamboyant of the Manchester textile warehouses

85 Canada House, built in 1909, was designed to be rented to many tenants

drafting department and main warehouse, which is why they were so huge, with seven storeys and 27 bays fronting Oxford Street encompassing 1000 rooms. The structure is faced in Portland stone in a Baroque style with a central pediment and tower over what has been described as the most elaborate entrance of any of the Manchester-style warehouses. To the rear the warehouses are stark, being dominated by huge window areas (Hartwell, Hyde & Pevsner 2004, 320-1; Parkinson-Bailey 2000, 137-8). The St James' Buildings were erected at the pinnacle of the Lancashire textile industry, at a time when large profits were being made from the 7 billion yards of cloth exported in 1913, manufactured in more than 2000 Lancashire cotton mills by 620,000 people. The complex was at the heart of the commercial district of the city, which at the time covered around one square mile of Manchester and arguably remains the finest expression of a Victorian and Edwardian commercial centre in Britain.

OTHER INDUSTRIES IN MANCHESTER

One of the great ironies of Manchester's industrial archaeology is that despite the longest building boom since Edwardian period, which has led to the archaeological recording of scores of warehouses and domestic dwellings, and the excavation of more than a dozen textile sites, we have yet to extensively investigate many of the city's lesser nineteenth-century manufacturing industries (*86*). Documentary records, maps and photographs record scores of sites across the city centre associated in this period with beer making, brick making, clay pipe manufacture and hatting. Virtually nothing remains standing of these sites and few have been excavated. In the early 1980s, the foundations of two small clay pipe kilns from the late eighteenth or early nineteenth centuries were excavated at Hurst Court off Long Millgate opposite Chethams School (Morris 1983, 58-9), whilst in 2003 an eighteenth- and nineteenth-century hat works was excavated on the northern

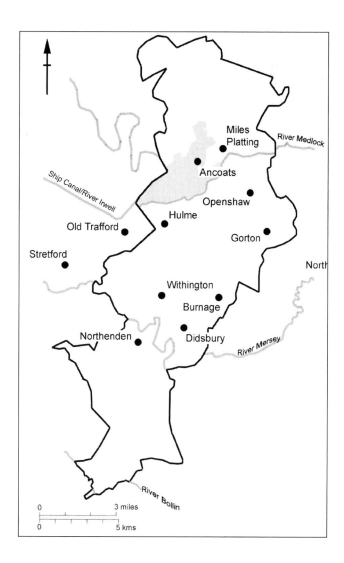

86 Manchester's nineteenth-century industrial suburbs

side of Hardman Street. Next to this site was a small soda works, for the manufacture and bottling of carbonated water. Here a well and the base of a wagon boiler, both important elements in the manufacturing process, were excavated. These excavated sites remain exceptional.

Whilst we know little about the physical remains of such support industries, two secondary industries are slightly better understood from an archaeological viewpoint: engineering and glass making. As cotton grew in importance and the canal and later the railway network around the city region developed, so Manchester led the way in new casting and wrought iron production techniques and in the building of machinery for the textile industry (Musson 1973, 55). This was how the Murray brothers and McConnel and Kennedy began their manufacturing careers in Manchester. From about 1780, Manchester firms were producing textile machinery, steam engines, waterwheels, boilers, mill gearing, iron pillars, beams and girders for mill building and bridges. Early engineering works within the city included Batemen and Sherratt's ironworks, established in the 1790s in Ancoats, and by 1850 there were 114 engineering and forge sites across the city. There are no surviving above-ground iron working and engineering sites in the centre of Manchester from this period. It is likely that smaller forge sites, several dozen of which are recorded in the city's earliest directories from 1772, 1788 and 1800, may await discovery in those parts of Manchester where dwellings and warehousing survive from this period.

Whilst all signs of the early nineteenth-century engineering works and forges within the city have gone, some of their finished products still survive, particularly those from two sources – the Bellhouse family, who came to specialise in mill construction, and William Fairbairn, Manchester's most noted engineer (87). David Bellhouse and Sons, builders, engineers and iron-founders, worked extensively around the city region from the 1820s onwards (Hartwell 2001, 217). They built the notorious six-storey cast iron-framed Islington Mill on Factory Lane in Salford in 1823 (Hartwell, Hyde & Pevsner 2004, 628). Its partial collapse in 1824 is credited with delaying the widespread introduction of this type of fireproof construction in the Manchester region. That did not stop the firm from building mills, and surviving examples in Manchester include Brunswick Mill from the 1840s (Williams with Farnie 1992, 79). Bellhouse was also the contractor for the more successful and better known 1830 Liverpool Road Warehouse. The family built other industrial structures such as cast iron railway and road bridges, and warehouses such as the canal warehouse at Portland Basin in Ashton erected in 1832-34 (Nevell & Walker 2001, 14). Their most obvious monument is the 224-arched viaduct for the Manchester South Junction and Altrincham Railway that links Piccadilly Station and Liverpool Road. The front of David Bellhouse Jr's Manchester town house of 1832 survives on Ormond Street

87 Cast iron columns, such as these supporting the viaduct servicing Central Station, opened in 1880, are often the only physical evidence left of Manchester's nationally important nineteenth-century engineering industry

on the western side of Grosvenor Square, on Oxford Road, which at the time was a fashionable suburb south of the city centre.

The most famous of Manchester's nineteenth-century engineers was William Fairbairn, whose first contract as a millwright in 1817 involved the replacement of line shafting in Murray's Mills (Williams with Farnie 1992, 70). He established an engineering works in Ancoats in the 1820s which has since been demolished. Its roof structure used cast iron trusses held under tension by wrought iron ties of the type that can still be seen at the 1824 Beehive Mill. Likewise, the iron roof he designed for the wholesale Smithfield Market in the Northern Quarter has gone (Hartwell 2001, 229, 284). His varied work survives all over the Manchester region from the undercroft at Bolton Market (1854) to Brunswick Mill in Ancoats. He developed innovatory designs for corn mills, waterwheels (an 1836 suspension waterwheel of Fairbairn's design can still be seen at the Portland Basin Canal Warehouse in Ashton-under-Lyne) and fireproofing in textile mills; one of the first mills he was involved in designing was the eight-storey Sedgewick Mill in Ancoats, and the replacement of the columns on all but the ground and first floors in 1865 was one of his last projects (Hartwell 2001, 279).

He is probably best known for his work with Eaton Hodgkinson, a Manchester scientist. The two of them worked on the design of cast iron beams, testing tensile stresses in Fairbairn's Ancoats works. Hodgkinson was able to design a beam that was lighter, stronger and cheaper than other beams, whilst Fairbairn's works tested and manufactured them. They had I-shaped cross-sections with a wider bottom flange and sides that formed a convex parabolic curve when viewed from below, making them quite distinctive. They were first used in 1830 in the construction of the now demolished, flat, level Water Street Bridge that carried the Liverpool and Manchester Railway. Their beams formed the basis for all future nineteenth-century structural cast iron design (Williams with Farnie 1992, 80) and were extensively used in textile mill design from the mid nineteenth century. In Manchester this can still be seen at the 1845 extension to Chorlton New Mill and at Fireproof Mill in Ancoats (Fitzgerald 1988). Hodgkinson was also one of the inventors of the Lancashire steam boiler, patented in 1844 with John Hetherington (Williams with Farnie 1992, 86), and probably of the north-light roof structure. His works supplied much of the iron work for the construction of Manchester mills from the 1820s to the 1850s and he was involved in the building of textile mills in Carlisle (Shaddon Mill from 1836) and the Saltaire woollen mill complex in Yorkshire in the 1850s.

After 1830, Manchester led the development of machine-tool production and precision engineering; physical remains from this period can still be seen around the city. The Castlefield Iron Works on Castle Street, also known as the Bass Warehouse, is a multi-storey structure, dating from around 1850, used for machine part manufacture. It survives along with its forge chimney and loading bays. The multi-storey Phoenix Works of Curtis and Sons on Chapeltown Street, which produced textile machinery parts, dates from around 1850, and the workshops of John Hetherington and Son's Vulcan Textile Works still stands on Pollard Street, where it was founded in 1856.

As space within the city centre became restricted in the late nineteenth century, engineering firms began to move to such outer districts as Gorton, Newton Heath, and Openshaw. Within this area was the extensive locomotive works of Beyer-Peacock. Although this complex has gone, lesser engineering sites survive. In 1898 Archibald Eva and his sons James and Joseph moved their forge works from Bradford to Crabtree Lane in Openshaw, where the company of Eva Brothers Ltd was still partially located when the forge works were taken over in 1990, the site finally closing in 2003. Shortly before this, the buildings and products were recorded by the Manchester Region Industrial Archaeology Society and form a rare record of a working engineering site in Manchester. The 19 buildings on the three acre site comprised a mixture of single-storey forges and erecting shops (the latter with overhead cranes), a warehouse and a two-storey office block, all with multi-light windows and steel trusses supporting glazed roofs. In 2003 the site still contained a forge with three gas furnaces and two forging hammers that had been converted to pneumatic operation.

Whilst archaeological research into the engineering industry in Manchester is at an early stage, the Manchester glass industry has been the subject of recent extensive study by members of the Manchester Region Industrial Archaeology Society, the University of Manchester and Oxford Archaeology North, prompted by the threat of redevelopment in the late 1990s and first few years of this century.

The first Manchester glassworks was recorded in 1795, whilst the last site, the Perseverance Glassworks of Redrick Hampson in Duncan Street, Salford, closed in 1964. So far a total of 25 flint glass works have been located operated by 39 different business partnerships in Manchester during this period. Many of the early firms were concerned with the manufacture of high quality free-blown, fine cut and engraved tablewares (Miller 2007, 15). The industry in the city was notable for its rapid expansion, in part resulting from the lifting of the Excise Tax on glasswares in 1845, and equally rapid decline due to the unregulated competition from overseas. By 1833 there were six firms listed in the local directory. The prosperity of the Manchester industry was based upon the introduction of the glass press during the 1850s, led by Percival Vickers & Co, who gradually shifted their production from blown glass to pressed glass in the late nineteenth century, so that the city rivalled Birmingham as a centre for this type of production in the period 1860-90 (Bone 2005). The distribution of glassworks in Manchester shows that the densest concentration was in the industrial suburb of Ancoats, which had seven sites, with a further eight located north-east of the city centre. Five works were located in Salford and three in Hulme. Such glass-making companies were dependent on the availability of cheap fuel, labour and an extensive reliable transport system to distribute their products (Champness & Nevell 2003).

The life of the Manchester glass industry spanned the transition from blown glass in glass cones to pressed glass made in rectangular kiln structures. Glass cones were developed in the mid eighteenth century and comprised a central furnace, heated from below, in which the glass was melted, whilst the glass makers worked in the circular space surrounding the furnace tending various side arches connected to the central hearth by flues or lunettes. The cone provided both the chimney draught for the furnace and a covered work space. They were usually 80ft high and up to 50ft wide at the base. Glass products were annealed (slowly cooled) at a controlled rate in the side arches of the furnace (Jones 1996, 162-3). The rectangular glass kiln performed the same function but was larger and so could accommodate the increasing demand for pressed glass from the early nineteenth century. It was this kind of kiln that dominated the Manchester glass industry.

The 2003 excavations of three kilns at the Percival Vickers & Co works in Jersey Street represents the first opportunity to investigate archaeologically this particular branch of Manchester's secondary industries. Historically the site was the largest glassworks in the city, working in the period 1844 to 1914. The history of this site has been studied by MRIAS and the surviving office and warehouse structures studied with the University of Manchester, whilst the excavations were undertaken by Oxford Archaeology North. Percival Yates & Vickers' flint glass works at 64 Jersey Street was established in 1844. By 1863, the Jersey Street works had 373 employees including 43 boys less than 13 years of age. By 1869, the maps suggest two kilns were in operation, rising to three by 1880, marking the peak of the company's fortunes (Bone 2005). The warehouse/office building range is the only part of the complex surviving above ground. It is a three-phased brick structure with three storeys and a roof of king-post trusses, braced by bolts, renovated in the late 1990s. Internally, it has wooden floors supported by cast iron columns and there was a cellar at the northern end of the range with a fireproof brick barrel-vaulted ceiling. The original 1844 building is probably represented by the southern 10 bays of the structure, with the two subsequent phases adding nine and then eight bays by 1880. There are various blocked doorways and windows at the southern end of the south-eastern elevation which may be connected with a number of the excavated structures to the rear (Champness & Nevell 2003).

The excavations uncovered three pot-type furnaces and an annealing house, and most importantly recorded variations in the design of the glass furnaces that demonstrated technological developments in the later nineteenth century previously unknown during this period. The two primary kilns, built in the 1840s, were 6.4m in diameter with furnace walls 0.5m thick surviving to a depth of 2m and were each capable of holding 10 pots. The core of each furnace was at foundation level 2.7m thick and each was encircled by a narrow brick-lined and flagstone-capped channel. The adjoining annealing house where the blown vessels were transferred to an oven for controlled cooling was also from this initial period. The third, most easterly, furnace was added in the 1870s and was more advanced technically (*88*). It was 7.16m in diameter, with exterior walls 0.84m thick and a furnace diameter of 4.6m and was again capable of holding 10 pots (Miller 2007. 19-24). All three kilns were reverbatory furnaces worked at the temperatures between 1400° and 1600°c needed to melt the raw materials and ensure that any gaseous bubbles formed during the melting process were eliminated. The air for combustion was drawn through two flues, a feature common to many other Manchester glassworks, but not often found elsewhere. Regulating the volume of air passing through the intake flue was an important part of the manufacturing process and was done by placing a shutter across the flue that would have been operated from the furnace floor. The third furnace shows evidence for the introduction of ceramic pipes in the siege area that would have allowed the combustion air to be preheated, whilst the introduction of a Frisbie feeder allowed a deeper and more consistently packed coal bed, so improving firing. Both innovations would have improved the thermal efficiency of the kiln.

These features are unique in this period and may explain why Percival Vickers was able to continue in production using pot-type furnaces at a time when the more fuel-efficient and thermal-efficient Siemens'-designed gas-fired furnace, which used a recycled heat system, became commonplace in the 1880s in the major glass-making centres of Birmingham and St Helens (Miller 2007, 27-8).

88 The late nineteenth-century glass kiln at the Jersey Street glassworks during excavation. This contained a number of innovative features only known during this period from archaeological excavations

THE WORLD'S FIRST INDUSTRIAL CITY

During the nineteenth century, Manchester emerged as one of Great Britain's leading cities and a focus for the industrialisation of society. It was at the centre and forefront of three industrial revolutions: an urban-based manufacturing revolution exemplified by the mills in Ancoats and Chorlton-on-Medlock; a transport revolution, typified by the Ashton and Rochdale Canals and their canal arms; and the first intercity mainline passenger railway with its terminus at Liverpool Road, and an engineering revolution, where advances in machine technology were pioneered by such people as William Fairbairn. The archaeology of this industrialised landscape remains extensive and exceptional, and is one of the greatest legacies that Manchester has given to the modern world.

CHAPTER 6

LIVING IN THE INDUSTRIAL CITY

Frederich Engels' description of Manchester is the best known and most debated of the many visitors' sketches of the city. Writing in 1842-43, but published later in his book 'The Condition of the Working Class in England', his descriptions of housing and living conditions within the city have become infamous. Engels concluded that the

> 350,000 working people of Manchester and its environs live, almost all of them, in wretched, damp, filthy cottages, that the streets which surround them are usually in the most miserable and filthy condition, laid out without the slightest reference to ventilation, with reference solely to the profit secured by the contractor
>
> Engels 1845

His comments came after more than 60 years of rapid urban and industrial expansion and at the end of a 20 year period when Manchester doubled its population size, but not its physical area. He was thus writing at the most acute period in Manchester's housing provision and at the peak of the overcrowding of this new industrial city. Yet his comments had been foreshadowed 50 years earlier by John Aikin writing in 1795:

> It [Manchester] unfortunately vies with, or exceeds, the metropolis, in the closeness with which the poor are crowded in offensive, dark, damp, and incommodious habitations, a too fertile source of disease!
>
> Aikin 1795, 192

The rapid factory-based industrialisation of the late eighteenth and early nineteenth century coincided with a phenomenal rise in population (*89*). Manchester nearly doubled its size between 1801 and 1821 from 75,281 to 126,066 people, and then more than doubling by 1851, when there were 303,382 people within the new borough (Hartwell 2001, 17). This new population required huge amounts of housing and between 1773 and 1821 the number of dwellings in the city rose from 3446 to 17,257 (Kidd 2002 38); by 1851 it had reached nearly 50,000 (*90*).

Until recently, few physical remains of workers' housing from this period were recognised within the city. Survey work in the 1980s and 1990s has rediscovered dozens

89 A view of Manchester from the north-west in 1795. At this date the city extended no further than the inner ring road of the early twenty-first century, but was home to nearly 70,000 people. Today this same area contains less than 15,000 people

of eighteenth-century houses and since 2001 more than a dozen excavations have revealed the remains of the slum dwellings built in the first half of the nineteenth century. For the first time archaeology is able to augment the contemporary accounts of social commentators such as Aikin, Kay and Engels with physical evidence, some of which shows such reports to be exaggerated, whilst other finds demonstrate that these reports underestimated the worse aspects of contemporary industrial housing. What has emerged from the archaeological evidence is a marked contrast between the workers' housing of the late eighteenth century and that of the first half of the nineteenth century, with the 1820s and 1830s being particularly notable for the poor quality of the houses built during these decades.

THE EIGHTEENTH–CENTURY WORKSHOP DWELLING

Research undertaken since the 1980s, firstly by the Manchester Early Dwellings Research Group and the Manchester Region Industrial Archaeology Society and since 1997 by the University of Manchester, has indicated that large numbers of eighteenth-century vernacular workshops, or as they are known locally, workshop dwellings, survive within the city centre (*91*). Such dwellings were characterised as being three-storeys high with a cellar and were usually one room or one bay deep. The upper, or attic, storey contained a

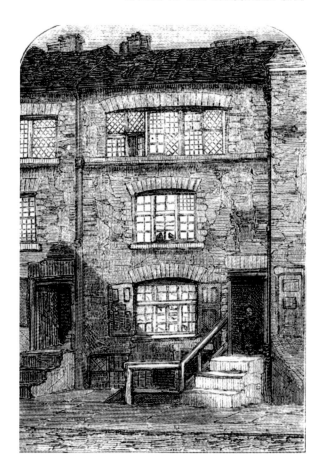

90 The exterior of one of
Manchester's workshop dwellings,
as published by *The Builder* in 1862.
By then this kind of dwelling had
declined into multiple-occupancy

workshop lit by long multi-light windows and the cellar was often also used as a workshop.
They were described as early as 1799 by Joshua Gilpin as being 'ab[ou]t 20 or 30 feet wide
composed of houses of three storeys above and one underground, not above 7ft 6ins or
8ft high …' (Roberts 1999, 2).

These workshop dwellings were the counterpart to the rural weaver's cottage and
documentary evidence shows that the hand-powered machinery contained in these
vernacular workshops was of two types: firstly looms, and later spinning jennies. The
invention in 1733 of the flying shuttle by John Kay enabled a weaver to sit centrally at
the loom and propel the shuttle through the warp from side to side by pulling buffers, or
pickers, along a slide rod in a box fixed to each end of the sley (Benson 1983, 9). It was a
significant factor in the growth of fustian production, particularly in Manchester itself.
Furthermore, this simple device greatly boosted the rate of hand loom production and
increased the need for a faster way of spinning.

The earliest practical machine for cotton spinning (that is the drawing out and twisting
of fibres to form a long thread) was the spinning jenny that was invented by James
Hargreaves in 1764. This was a multi-spindle machine that drafted and twisted the cotton
in one stage and wound it onto a spindle in a second stage. The whole process was initially

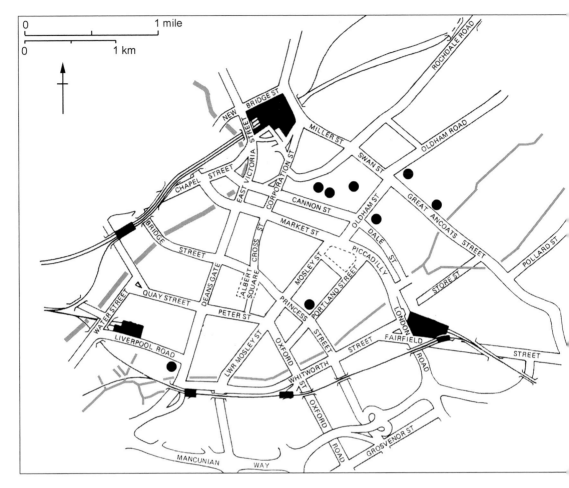

91 The main areas of surviving workshop dwellings within the city centre

hand-driven via a wheel on a machine that initially had eight spindles and could be housed in a workshop dwelling, but in its most developed form in the early nineteenth century, the jenny had as many as 120 spindles and could be steam-powered (Benson 1983, 12). The yarn produced was soft and thick, rather than having a consistently hard twist, but for the cotton industry was ideal for use as weft, which is probably why the hand-powered jenny remained in popular use as late as the patenting of the self-acting mule in 1830 (Jones 1996, 249-50). Jennies could be housed in existing buildings such as barns in rural locations (Nevell & Walker 1998) or vernacular workshops in the town (*92*). Thus, advertisements in the *Manchester Mercury* newspaper during the 1780s refer to houses for sale or rent that were suitable for conversion to workshops and from the 1790s mentions premises suitable for jenny spinning (Little 2007, 15-6). How prevalent the jenny was in the vernacular workshops of Manchester before the 1780s is unclear.

Of all the areas of new housing built on the fringes of eighteenth-century Manchester, one area in particular came to be dominated by the workshop dwelling; the new police watch district know as St Paul's. The St Paul's district was one of 14 special constable districts that had developed by 1800 as the town more than trebled in size during the eighteenth century. It lay to the north-east of the medieval core of Manchester within the present Northern Quarter and was defined by the following streets: on the east by Lever Street, on the north by Great Ancoats Street and Swan Street, on the west by Shudehill, Nicholas Croft and High Street, and on the south by Market Street and Piccadilly. Map evidence indicates that the street pattern of this roughly rectangular zone has remained largely intact since the eighteenth century. The two main thoroughfares running north to south were Oldham Street and Lever Street, whilst the Church Street/Dale Street and Thomas Street/ Hilton Street alignments provided east to west access through the area (Nevell 2003).

Three eighteenth-century maps of Manchester indicate how rapidly this part of the town developed in the second half of the eighteenth century. The earliest Casson and Berry's map of Manchester from around 1740 shows that only the south-western quarter of the St Paul's district had been developed by this date, with only two of the four roads that later delineated the district shown. High Street is shown as having housing on both sides as far north as its junction with Shudehill and houses are shown along the northern

92 Workshop dwellings on Liverpool Road, built between 1788 and 1794

side of Market Street as far east as the River Tib. Within this area, Garden Lane, Church Street and Turner Street are shown running eastwards from High Street, though there are large gaps in the housing in this area, which did not extend as far as the River Tib. St Paul's church itself was absent.

Tinker's map of Manchester, published in 1772 as part of the town's first directory, shows that housing in this area had grown to cover over a third of the district (*93 & 94*). In particular Garden Lane, Church Street and Turner Street, at the end of which St Paul's church was built in 1765 (Hartwell 2001, 11), now ran as far east as the River Tib and smaller north-south roads had been built such as Birchin Lane and Union Street. Housing extended northwards on both sides of Shudehill as far north as its junction with Millers Lane. North of St Paul's church and east of the River Tib there was no housing, though the line of Oldham Street was marked as an intended street showing that it was

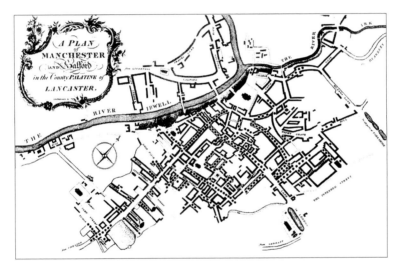

93 The distribution of people involved in textile occupations from the first Manchester trade directory of 1772

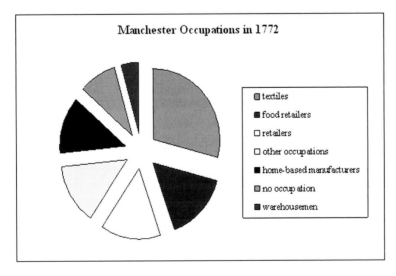

94 A breakdown of trade occupations as recorded in the Manchester's trade directory of 1772. Textile manufacturing predominates and at this date would have been all domestic hand production

part of the development of the area to the east of St Paul's church by the Lever family, who had begun to sell land for building in this area in the early 1770s (Hartwell 2001).

According to Green's map of Manchester, published in 1794, nearly all of the St Paul's district had been built upon. The eastern boundary of this area, the newly built Oldham Street, faced a rectilinear grid of streets focused upon Stevenson's Square that ran to the south-east. Behind Oldham Street, the vast majority of St Paul's district was characterised by an irregular street pattern, with many narrow alleyways and courtyards, especially along Tib Street and Back Turner Street corridors. The exception was the corner of the district bordering the junction of Shudehill and Swan Street, where there remained large areas of open space and only a few isolated houses.

An analysis of the 1800 directory for Manchester indicates that the character of the St Paul's district was that of a mixed working class residential, commercial and manufacturing district. Of the 114 people listed as resident in the St Paul's district, the largest single grouping were textile workers and manufacturers, with 23.9 per cent of the entries, home-based manufacturing workers accounted for 21 per cent, followed by food retailers at 15.7 per cent, retailers at 6.8 per cent, those with no occupation at 6 per cent and warehousemen at 5 per cent. Other occupations accounted for 21.6 per cent of the entries. By 1800, most of the St Paul's district was covered in small-scale vernacular workshop dwellings and examples of these can still be found along Tib Street, Thomas Street and Turner Street (Hartwell 2001). There were small-scale Georgian town houses on Oldham Street and warehouses in Red Lion Street and Birchin Street. There were even a number of factories – along Oak Street two steam-powered cotton spinning mills are recorded by 1795 (Little 2007, 21).

Six examples of these late eighteenth-century vernacular workshops have been studied in detail within a block formed by Turner Street, Kelvin Street (formerly Milk Street), Back Turner Street and Brick Street. This block of land appears to have been divided into plots that were sold during the 1740s and 1750s by a merchant called Josiah Nicholls, to 17 individuals. Green's map of 1794 indicates that virtually the whole of this block was built on by 1794. The three directories published between 1772 and 1800 indicate that these streets contained a variety of properties. Turner Street was dominated by the houses of manufacturers who had their business elsewhere, whilst the properties on Milk Street and Back Turner Street were occupied by craftsmen or tradesmen who lived and worked in the same buildings. Occupations mentioned in the trade directories from this period included timber, flour and tea dealers and sellers, as well as joinery, shoemaking and textiles (Nevell 2003).

The earliest of the six vernacular workshop dwellings studied is No. 36 Back Turner Street, built in the period 1755-57. The title deeds analysed by the Manchester Early Dwellings Research Group show it was part of four blocks of land bought by Peter Hall, a slater, and like many of the other 17 individuals to whom land was sold in this block, Mr Hall was probably a speculative builder. Its three floors and cellar covered an area of 81m². No. 37 Turner Street was probably built in the 1760s and was certainly no later than 1772-73, though by whom is unknown. The cellar retained the railed area along Turner Street and the whole had a floor area of 198m². Nos 1-5 Milk Street were erected in the

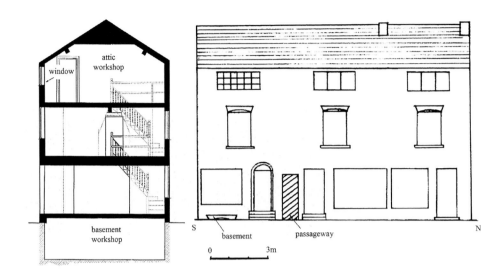

95 Elevation and section of the Milk (Kelvin) Street workshop dwellings. These were built in 1772-3 by Mr and Mrs Manchester, fustian manufacturers, and had shared attic work spaces

years 1772-73 and had floor areas of 110m², 129m² and 115m². No. 38 Back Turner Street was erected in the years 1794-1800 on part of the plot bought by Peter Hall in 1755 and had a floor area of 110m² (Nevell 2005).

The title deeds and early rate books are most revealing as regards the late eighteenth-century history of Nos 1-5 Milk Street (95). These three properties were built by Richard and Mary Manchester in 1772-73 and let by that family until sold by them in 1790s (Nevell 2003). Directory evidence indicates that the family were textile traders. The only Manchester family member mentioned in the 1772 directory was a Richard Manchester, who was described as a cow-keeper resident on Great Turner Street, just a few streets away from Milk Street. The 1788 directory records one Manchester family member, again a Richard, who was described as a dealer and chapman (that is a textile merchant) of Red Bank. The 1800 directory lists two Manchesters – another Richard resident at 68 Bank Top and a Benjamin who was described as a twist dealer with a house at 81 Hanover Street. It seems likely that at least some of these people were either the same individuals or part of the same family as those mentioned in the deeds to the Milk Street properties from 1772. Unfortunately no tenants are known before the 1790s, thereafter residents include fustian weavers. The building of a row of three workshop dwellings, such as those at Nos 1-5 Milk Street, by Richard Manchester, would seem to fit into a pattern of semi-domestic textile manufacture that typified the putting-out system controlled by the chapmen of eighteenth-century Manchester.

The layout of the three Milk Street properties shows they were built as a single working unit by the Manchester family. Internally, the ground and first floors of each property acted as the domestic areas, each floor being heated and perhaps divided by

96 Workshop dwellings at Nos 49 to 53 Tib Street were built in the period 1783 to 1794 and had shared attic and basement workshops

a wooden screen, and provided a total living area of 50m². Below was a cellar accessed only from the individual property, but each third floor attic room was connected to the others, providing three linked workspaces with a taking-in door at the rear of the northern-most attic room. On the ground floor, a covered passageway between the southern and middle properties led to the rear enclosed courtyard and the area below the taking-in door. Elsewhere within the Northern Quarter, Nos 49 to 53 Tib Street provides another well preserved example of a set of vernacular workshop dwellings, though there is no documentary evidence to indicate who built them (96). They comprised a set of four properties built on the western side of Tib Street in three phases between 1783 and 1794. These were slightly more developed than the Milk Street range, with the basement work areas linked by internal doorways and the second floor attic space converted into a single workshop. Furthermore, there was a large rear wing with a third-floor taking-in door and hoist that appears to have acted as a dedicated warehouse. A George Kendal was recorded at No. 51 Tib Street in Banck's directory of Manchester from 1800, but no occupation was given, and a Christopher Wadsworth, a shoemaker, at No. 53. However, it is not certain that these properties had the same house numbers as those recorded today, and even if they did, it is possible that the attic workshop was run separately from the domestic accommodation below.

Both these sets of vernacular workshops are listed and have been renovated and restored in recent years. The redevelopment of the city centre since 1996 has given the opportunity to excavate several further examples. The fragmentary basement remains of a set of three separate vernacular workshops built before 1794 were excavated on the southern side of Copperas Street in 2004, revealing deep, well-built foundations with unheated basements. In 2005 the Channel 4 archaeology programme *Time Team* excavated, with the help of the University of Manchester, a single vernacular workshop on the southern side of Angel Street. Part of the front room and the whole of a rear room were excavated, giving a floor area of roughly 5.4m by 4.3m. A halfpenny was found encased in mortar from the cellar backfill with the date 1775 inscribed, suggesting these

97 The basements of two workshop dwellings during excavations at Southern Street. These were built in the period 1788-94

properties were built around this date. They were first shown on a map of Manchester from 1788. The front room had a flagstone floor, which might have been later, but the rear room had an original handmade brick floor and both spaces were originally heated. Bancks' directory of 1800 records a Michael Smith, shoemaker, at 39 Angel Street, which is a candidate for the site of the excavation.

The best preserved examples of vernacular workshop basements were excavated in 2005 on Southern Street (97). These belonged to properties built before 1788 and each was divided into a front, western room measuring 5m by 3.7m and a rear, eastern room measuring 5m by 2.7m. The front rooms were floored with rectangular Yorkstone flags, but a coin from below the flags of 1875 indicated that the floor had been re-laid in at least one property. The original floor levels did survive within both rear rooms in the form of a series of red handmade bricks laid unbonded on their sides, stretcher to stretcher. Each front room had a 1m-wide fireplace or range built into the southern wall, whilst the rear rooms had smaller 0.75m wide fireplaces. A doorway leading onto Southern Street was excavated at the northern end of each front wall, which was 0.85m wide and had timber jambs still extant. A similar doorway was found in the dividing wall of each basement. The extremely limited finds excavated from these two basements included unglazed earthenwares, dark-glazed earthenwares, stoneware, transfer-printed wares from plates and pancheons (dishes) of the late eighteenth and early nineteenth centuries, suggesting that these basements had always been used as storage or domestic areas.

Nearby were a row of eight extant individual, three-storey vernacular workshop dwellings from the same period, Nos 29 to 43 Liverpool Road (Hartwell 2001, 270) (*98*). Each had basements and long casement windows to their third floors and this range indicates the original form of the Southern Street dwellings. Detailed study of No. 37 Liverpool Road by the Manchester Region Industrial Archaeology Society in 2006 indicated that unlike the Milk Street and Tib Street examples, these properties remained as individual workshop dwellings. The properties appear to have been built in pairs, beginning with Nos 29 and 31, 33 and 35, then 37 and 39, followed by Nos 41 and 43. This development seems to have taken place during the years 1788-94. No. 37 had four

98 Detail of the elevation of two of the Liverpool Road workshop dwellings showing the long attic windows. Such buildings were often erected by speculative builders in rows of two, three or four properties

open floors with areas of 30.4m², including the original remains of two flights of stairs and their banister rails, giving a total floor space of 121.6m² including the cellar; comparable to the Milk Street examples. Unlike those properties it also had its own rear yard and outside privy by 1794. Although the builders of these properties are unknown, Banck's 1800 directory lists a number of people potentially involved in home-based production in this area including a cutler and a joiner on Priestner Street (later Liverpool Road), whilst in the adjoining Southern Street there was a shoemaker and one William Hilditch, a fustian cutter, thus demonstrating the presence of hand-based textile manufacture in this area at the turn of the century.

THE EMERGENCE OF SLUM DWELLINGS IN MANCHESTER

Whilst the vernacular workshop dwelling represented on the whole good quality eighteenth-century artisan housing, by the end of the century the rapid industrialisation of Manchester had begun to lead to a decline in housing standards and a sharp rise in population densities (*99*). These would culminate in the appalling slum conditions recorded by Engels, Kay, Reach and other social commentators during the 1830s and 1840s. John Aikin was probably the first to detail these problems, noting in 1795 that 'in some parts of the town, cellars are so damp as to be unfit for Habitations; … I have known several industrious families lost to the community, by a short residence in damp cellars' (Aikin 1795, 193). When the poet and historian Robert Southey visited Manchester in 1808 he was less than impressed with both the way the mills were worked and with the housing conditions of the mill hands:

> The dwellings of the labouring manufacturers are in narrow streets and lanes, blocked up from light and air … crowded together because every inch of land is of such value, that room for light and air cannot be afforded them.
>
> Bradshaw 1987, 24

These and other nineteenth-century commentaries can now be amplified by more than a dozen recent excavations around Manchester and Salford (*100*). This growing body of excavated domestic dwellings includes early nineteenth-century back-to-back housing from Barton Street and Southern Street, both in Castlefield; the same type of house but terraced, at Liverpool Road, White Lion Street, Quay Street and Syer's Court in Piccadilly, and excavated examples in the centre of Salford, opposite Manchester Cathedral, at Greengate and Rylands. In Ancoats, the world's first industrial suburb, early nineteenth-century back-to-back houses have been excavated on Bradley Street and the Victoria Works, late eighteenth-century terraced workers' housing excavated at the junction of Bengal Street and Jersey Street, and more than 22 houses spanning the late eighteenth to the late nineteenth centuries on Loom Street.

The very first workers' housing excavated in Manchester was on White Lion Street in Castlefield. These were explored by Professor Barri Jones as part of the 1972 Deansgate

MANCHESTER CELLAR DWELLINGS

Entrance to an Underground Shop: Cellars for Buyers.

A A. Entrance to Cellar Dwellings. No other Opening.

Interior of a Cellar Shop: Business and the Family.

Access to other Cellar Dwellings: Death in the Dirt.

99 Images of slum cellar dwellings as recorded in *The Builder* from 1862

Roman dig, the irony being that they were found as part of the exploration of the Roman vicus in front of the northern gateway. Professor Jones and his team took time to record the foundations of these back-to-back and blind-back houses from around 1825 (Jones & Grealey 1974, 79-80). None of the properties had cellars, though both the blind-backs on the northern side of White Lion Street and the back-to-back and through-houses on the southern side had back yards of varying sizes. The properties on the southern side of the street were accessed via a rear alleyway and the back-to-backs in this area may have formed a court development off White Lion Street. Some of these features can be seen on an aerial photograph of the area from 1947, which shows that all the houses had two storeys. Two characteristics emerged from these excavations that have been seen on several later sites – the lack of nineteenth-century finds and the shallow foundations, in this case only two and three bricks deep.

It was nearly 20 years before further workers' housing was excavated in Manchester. Again this was in Castlefield and they were recorded as part of a study of the Roman

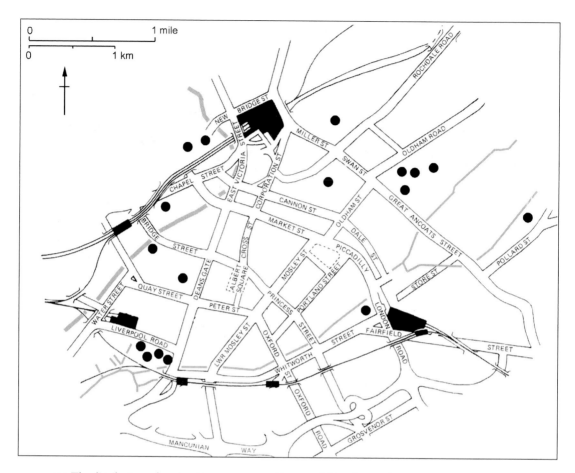

100 The distribution of workers' houses excavated in central Manchester since 2001

vicus. The excavations in 2001 off Liverpool Road revealed further properties erected in the 1820s, including a public house with cellars; the terraces of two-storey, two-roomed houses in Wood Street and Ball Street were not cellared. Artefacts and evidence for outside privies were scarce. The workers' houses excavated in 2005 at Barton Street and Worsley Street spanned the period 1788-94 to the 1820s. The earliest properties were a pair of workshop dwellings fronting Worsley Street with half-cellars each divided into two rooms, a northern or front cellar, of 3.7m by 4m and a back or southern cellar of 2.7m by 4m. The housing from the 1820s comprised two double-depth structures, facing the southern side of Worsley Street and each with a cellar *c.*2.7m deep. The smaller of the two buildings had a stone flagged floor whilst the larger had a brick floor with a brick oven. Just 87 sherds of pottery were associated with this housing and most of these came from two late eighteenth- and early nineteenth-century drains, with only a single backyard pit producing one dark-glazed rim sherd from the late eighteenth century.

The first excavations specifically targeted at workers' housing were those at Hardman Street in 2003, although the remains of the eighteenth- and early nineteenth-century workers' housing recovered was very fragmentary, unlike the remains of the hat factory and the adjacent soda works. The late eighteenth-century two-up two-down terraced housing excavated at Rylands in Salford and the early nineteenth-century housing on Greengate was very fragmentary, although at Greengate the remains of four blind-backs built in the 1820s were recovered (*101*). These were one-up one-down houses and represented the lowest form of housing in the city. The only known examples left standing are those in Bradley Street from the late 1780s, though these have been recently completely rebuilt. The Greengate examples had room sizes of less than 3.5m square with foundations of one brick depth, and whilst each ground floor room had a fireplace, there were no signs of any floor covering nor of a staircase and it is likely that the upper storey was accessed via a ladder.

In contrast, the remains of Syer's court off Minshull Street at Piccadilly excavated in 2004 revealed the deeply stratified and well-preserved remains of a set of seven back-to-back houses dating from the period 1831-36. These had heated half-cellars that in places still stood to a height of 1.4m, with steps into the rooms, partition walls one brick thick and flagged floors. The six back-to-back houses excavated at the Victoria Works site in 2006, between Armitage Street and Back Munday Street, were built during the peak period of house building in the city, the 1820s, in two phases, 1818-24 and 1824-31 and were physically separated by a paved alleyway (*102*). These were very well preserved because the half-cellared ground floors, *c*.3.75m by 4.3m, had been buried by a considerable overburden. There was a marked difference between the standard of construction between the two phases of houses, the later houses being of a much poorer standard. The foundations of the earliest houses were two bricks wide and the cellars flagged, whilst the foundations of the later houses were one brick wide and the cellars had a brick floor. There was a lack of artefacts from secure contexts.

These excavations show the range of housing erected in the city between 1780 and 1850, the peak period for the expansion of the population of the town. Of these properties the most notorious were the cellar dwellings and the back-to-back houses. Whilst significant numbers of converted cellar dwellings survive within the city centre, particularly in the Northern Quarter, there are no known examples of back-to-back housing left within Manchester. The only set of back-to-back houses to be recorded archaeologically, and the last to be demolished, were Walker's Buildings, Nos 7 to 29 Whittle's Croft, on the western edge of Ancoats (*103*). A detailed recording of these dwellings in 1990 (Sanders 1991) showed they were built in three main phases. The earliest houses were three pairs of back-to-back terraced cottages, with rooms of 3.4m by 4m, erected in the 1820s. A second block of two pairs of back-to-backs were built on to the southern gable of the original block in the 1830s and a pair of side-to-backs, with rooms of 4.2m by 4m, added to the southern end of these in the 1840s (*104*). They remained as dwellings until 1896 when the 12 houses were converted into workshops. This conversion process involved the replacement of much of the roof structure, the blocking of windows, and the removal of most of the internal walls.

Three houses survived largely intact. The earliest of these was No. 7 in the north-western corner of the block, dating from the 1820s, where just two handmade brick partition walls one brick wide survived, though there was a small fireplace against the

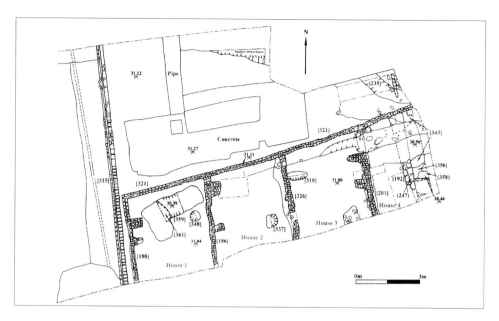

101 Plan of a set of found blind-back houses on Greengate in Salford, opposite St Mary's, Manchester. These were two-roomed cottages with windows only at the front and represented the poorest type of individual housing within Manchester. The foundations were no more than two bricks deep

102 The foundations of back-to-back houses at the Victoria Works in Ancoats, dating from the period 1818-31

northern gable and a blocked doorway and window in the western wall. A staircase against the eastern side of the eastern partition wall indicated where the original access to the upper rooms lay. The other two survivals were the side-to-backs, Nos 27 and 29 Whittle's Croft, at the southern end of the range, dating from the 1840s. These were more complete, with one-brick-wide partition walls covered in lime plaster containing two back-to-back brick chimney stacks for a fireplace in each room. The ground floor retained some of its original brick flooring and an original wooden staircase in the south-western corner of No. 27. At first floor level, the softwood floorboards and joists survive along with part of the roof structure, indicating that the upper rooms were open to the roof. Enough of the range of buildings survived to allow a reconstruction of the original floor plan. Each back-to-back house shared a pair of brick chimney stacks whilst on the ground floor was a door and a single window. The staircases were located against the central spine wall, except for those in the side-to-backs. The upper rooms were heated, lit by a single window and open to the roof space.

EAST ELEVATION

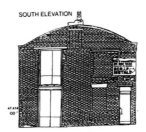

SOUTH ELEVATION

WALKER'S BUILDINGS

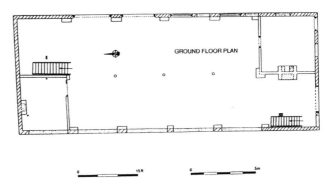

GROUND FLOOR PLAN

103 Elevations and ground-floor plan of Walker's Building, Whittle's Croft, Ancoats. These were the last known, surviving back-to-back houses when they were demolished in 1990 (*Image courtesy of GMAU*)

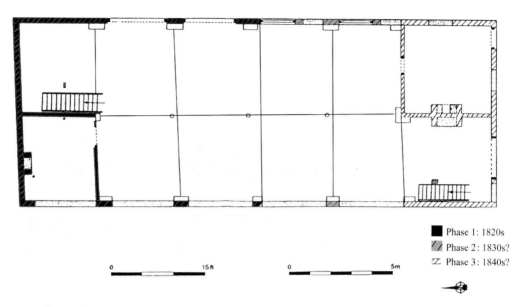

Phase 1: 1820s
Phase 2: 1830s?
Phase 3: 1840s?

0 _____ 15 ft   0 _____ 5m

104 Suggested original layout and phasing of Walker's Buildings (*Image courtesy of GMAU*)

LIVING IN NINETEENTH–CENTURY ANCOATS

Most of the recent excavations of workers' housing in Manchester have recorded two, three or four individual properties. Excavations at Loom Street, Ancoats, in the autumn of 2007, exposed more than 22 dwellings (Gregory 2007b) (*105*). This represents the largest archaeological investigation of late eighteenth- and nineteenth-century workers' housing within the city (*106*). In many respects, the excavations at Loom Street represent a microcosm of the early to mid nineteenth century industrial development within Manchester and not just Ancoats. Housing types recorded included back-to-back houses, blind-back houses, cellar dwellings, double-depth houses and domestic workshops. During the early nineteenth century the population expansion of the city led to vacant areas between the established housing stock being infilled with new worker's dwellings, which were often back-to-back and blind-back properties accessed only by narrow alleyways. This period also saw a more intensive occupation of the older housing stock, with the creation of cellar dwellings. As a result the Ancoats' population steadily increased from 11,039 in 1801 to 55,983 in 1861 (Roberts 1993, 16). These trends in population density became particularly noticeable following an increase in rents between 1807 and 1815 (Miller 2007, 31). This period of increased housing pressure was followed in the later nineteenth century by a slow improvement in housing quality through the addition of back yard privies, the closure of cellar dwellings and the demolition of some of the worst type of housing.

The map sources indicate that the area bounded by George Leigh, Bengal, Sherratt and Blossom Street was developed during the late eighteenth century through the

105 An aerial view of the western end of the block of land at Loom Street, Ancoats, where 22 dwellings were excavated in 2007

construction of double-depth and blind-back properties. The impetus was the early industrialisation of the area, which included the establishment of numerous textile mills concentrated along Union Street (Miller 2007, 28).

The largest of these properties were found fronting George Leigh Street and were exposed during the excavation of Area A and D. These properties measured *c*.5.5m wide (Houses D2-3) close to the corner of George Leigh and Bengal Street, narrowing to *c*.4.7m wide further along George Leigh Street (Houses D3 & A1). Each of the properties was provided with half-basements and raised ground floors. One of the excavated basements (House D1) contained a fireplace. An unexcavated house fronting Bengal Street was associated with a square brick built outshut, the remains of which were exposed in Area D. Though the function of this outshut is not entirely clear, it is possible that it was subdivided into individual privies, which were shared by the inhabitants of the double-depth houses. The recovery of architectural pieces from a porticoed doorway of one of the houses, together with the comparatively large internal areas, indicate that these properties were originally constructed as higher status dwellings. Indeed, it is possible that during this period these dwellings housed artisans, as was the case with a larger late eighteenth-century property found in nearby

106 The Loom Street area in 1849, showing the back-to-back houses, courts and cellar dwellings in this part of Ancoats. The excavation trenches are shaded and lettered

Sherratt Street, which contemporary rate books and trade directories indicate was occupied by a shoemaker during the early nineteenth century (Hradil *et al* 2007).

The properties (Houses B1-2, B4-5) found close to the corner of Loom and Sherratt Street were slightly smaller in size, measuring 4.5m wide by 7m deep, though were probably of a similar status to those flanking George Leigh Street. These properties differed in one major respect in that they did not have basements. Instead the remains of two of these houses (Houses B4 & B5) indicate that each property was composed, at ground level, of two 3.5m-deep rooms. In the rear rooms of houses B4 and B5, which would have been positioned behind the parlour, the remains of fireplaces attached to the eastern partition walls were identified. An outshut was also exposed, linked to the rear of house B4, which may have functioned as a shared privy.

The houses (Houses E1-3) excavated at the eastern end of Loom Street were smaller in size and were presumably of lower status than the eighteenth-century houses fronting Loom and George Leigh Street. As with the larger properties found at the western end of Loom Street, these properties did not have basements. The remains indicate that each house measured 4m wide by 6.5m deep and was composed of a *c*.2.8m-deep rear room and a larger 3.7m-deep front room. Within the rear room of the properties were fireplaces and flights of stairs allowing access to the first floor.

The smallest late eighteenth-century houses were the blind-back properties located at the corner of George Leigh and Sherratt Street. It was not possible to fully excavate these houses. However, it was established that they were provisioned with half-basements and an outshut was linked to one of these properties, which may have functioned as a shared privy. A late eighteenth-century blind-back house was partially exposed at the eastern end of Loom Street (House E4), which again appears to have been associated with an outshut that probably functioned as a shared privy.

The most common house type excavated at Loom Street was the back-to-back dwelling. The earliest examples were constructed between 1787-94 and 1818-19 and fronted both George Leigh Street and Jepson's Court, but were accessed from Loom Street (*107*). These houses had half-basements that contained fireplaces on their eastern walls. One property (House C2) measured internally 4.1m by 4m, whilst another (House C1) measured 3.9m by 3.9m. Access into the individual basements was via ladders leading from a trapdoor, which opened at ground level within each of the dwellings above. There was no evidence for cellar lights for the properties found fronting Jepson's Court, indicating that if these basements were occupied, the living conditions would have been particularly oppressive as they were not lit by natural light or adequately ventilated.

The back-to-back houses (Houses F1-3) excavated in the southern portion of the development area were probably constructed during the same period. Like the examples on George Leigh Street and Jepson's Court, these back-to-back dwellings fronted a major street – Blossom Street – and a smaller courtyard that was accessed via an alleyway off it – Blossom Court. The houses were similar in size, measuring *c*.3.9m by 3.9m, and had half-basements, which were probably accessed in the early nineteenth century via ladders leading from a trapdoor found at ground floor level. The basements contained fireplaces that had clearly been utilised due to the discovery of an ash pit and cast iron grate. In contrast to those found to the north, these half-basements were provisioned with cellar lights allowing the basements to be partially ventilated and lit by natural light.

Between 1831 and 1845, a further area of back-to-back housing was constructed on a previously empty plot of land (*108*). These houses fronted three separate courts but did not have any basements.

A number of double-depth houses were excavated on this site. Early nineteenth-century examples were examined at the western end of Loom Street and none of these were associated with basements. The rear portion of the properties (Houses G1-4) fronted the southern side of Loom Street and each property was *c*.3.8m wide by 6.2m deep containing two 3.1m deep rooms. The remains indicate that the rear rooms of the dwellings had a fireplace, situated on the eastern wall, whilst the stairs leading to the first floor were probably located in the front room. This arrangement directly contrasts with the one found in the late eighteenth-century houses fronting the eastern end of Loom Street (Houses E1-4), where the fireplace was located on the western wall, with the stairs leading to the first floor in the rear room of the dwelling.

107 Back-to-back houses in Area C, Loom Street, dating from 1794-1819

108 Back-to-back houses in Area G, Loom Street, dating from 1831-48. These were built as part of one of the many court developments in the city during this period

Several late eighteenth- and early nineteenth-century double-depth houses were excavated. One on the northern side of Loom Street (House B3) had been badly damaged internally by late alterations; it was *c*.3.8m wide and contained two separate properties that both had fireplaces. Some of the half-basements of the double-depth properties fronting George Leigh Street were used for non-domestic purposes. This was evident in the property (House A1) found close to the corner of George Leigh and Sherratt Street, whose basement was substantially modified during the mid nineteenth century through the insertion of two ovens.

It is possible that the basement of a house found to the east (House D1) was used as a workshop or conceivably during the late eighteenth/early nineteenth century as an area for domestic weaving and/or spinning. In this basement a metal fitting was found, which perhaps secured a craft worker's machine or tool. During the mid nineteenth century, a cellar light was inserted, allowing natural light to enter this area as well as ventilation.

In the 1840s, Frederick Engels visited Ancoats as part of his investigation into the conditions of the working classes. During this visit he considered the construction of the workers' houses in this area and commented that,

> ... on closer examination, it becomes evident that the walls of these cottages are as thin as it is possible to make them. The outer walls, those of the cellar, which bear the weight of the ground-floor and roof, are one whole brick thick at most ...
>
> Engels 1845

The excavated remains indicate that Engels' descriptions were not wholly applicable to the Loom Street area of Ancoats. For example, within the excavated areas, the majority of the workers' houses were constructed of two-course-thick external walls, with one-course-wide dividing/party walls, whilst some were surprisingly well constructed, such as the late eighteenth-century blind-back houses found at the corner of George Leigh Street and Sherratt Street, which were constructed of two- and three-course-wide brick walls. A number of these properties survived into the latter half of the twentieth century, though some suffered from serious structural problems. This was apparent in those excavated double-depth houses fronting Loom Street, where the internal walls of some of the houses had subsided due to inadequate foundations.

The conditions of many of the residents occupying worker's housing in Ancoats during the early to mid nineteenth century can be recovered from contemporary descriptions compiled by the middle classes. The more important of these, and which are relevant to the houses excavated at Loom Street, describe the conditions within No.1 District of Ancoats and have been summarised by Roberts (1993, 18-21). As early as 1819, the social fabric of Ancoats was viewed with trepidation (Roberts 1993, 18) and the low standard of living continued into the 1830s, highlighted in the surveys made by Kay and Gaulter in 1832. These surveys indicate that much worker's housing lacked common sewers, were not provisioned with privies and were badly ventilated, damp and filthy. A large proportion of the properties also appear to have been densely occupied by multiple families, who often occupied the basements with little in the way of basic facilities, such as bedding.

By the mid nineteenth century, contemporary descriptions suggest that living conditions had improved slightly. Engels (1845), for example, writing in 1844 notes that

> Farther to the north-east lie many newly-built-up streets; here the cottages look neat and cleanly, doors and windows are new and freshly painted, the rooms within newly whitewashed; the streets themselves are better aired, the vacant building lots between them larger and more numerous. But this can be said of a minority of the houses only, while cellar dwellings are to be found under almost every cottage; many streets are unpaved and without sewers.

A more detailed description of living conditions is provided by Angus Reach, who in 1849 described 'the generic features of the tenements in the older, worse built, and in all respects inferior quarters of Ancoats' (Aspin 1972, 6), including a description of the material culture that was often found within these houses. This description outlines two different types of mid nineteenth-century domestic life in Ancoats. His initial description appears to relate to the parlour, or front room, of a higher status worker's dwelling where

> … you have … an easy opportunity of noting the interiors as you pass along. They are, as you will perceive, a series of little rooms, about ten feet by eight, more or less, generally floored with brick and flagstone – materials which are, however, occasionally half concealed by strips of mats or faded carpeting. A substantial deal table stands in the centre of each apartment, and a few chairs, stools, and settles to match, are ranged around. Sometimes there is a large cupboard, the open door of which reveals a shining assortment of plates and dishes; sometimes the humble dinner service is ranged on shelves which stretch along the walls; while beneath them are suspended upon hooks a more or less elaborate series of skillets, stewpans, and miscellaneous cooking and household matters.
>
> Aspin 1972, 6–7

Reach continued by describing a cruder and lower status cellar dwelling in which

> The cellars are, as might be expected, seldom furnished so well. They appear to possess none of the minor comforts, none of the little articles of ornaments or fancy furniture which more or less you observe in the parlours. The floors seem damp and unwholesome, you catch a glimpse of a rickety-looking bed in a dark airless corner, and the fire upon the hearth is often cheerlessly small, smouldering amongst the unswept ashes.
>
> Aspin 1972, 7

The archaeological excavations at Loom Street (Gregory 2007b) have largely confirmed these descriptions through the recovery of 1024 finds, of which 779 were pottery sherds, representing 527 individual vessels. The pottery recovered from the excavations included utilitarian earthenwares used in the kitchen, stoneware vessels used in the pantry or cellar for cold storage, and fine porcelains and whitewares used at the table. One house in Area F produced a rubbish pit from the 1820s containing high quality pottery such as creamwares and fine porcelains (*109*). Other elements of material culture recovered during the excavation included glass and stoneware bottles, showing the consumption of mineral water, carbonated cordials or ginger beer by the working class population of Ancoats (*110*). These beverages were often drunk in preference to the local well water that was frequently contaminated. Of the dozens of stoneware sherds recovered, four types of stamps were apparent; one from a Glasgow maker and three from Manchester, but most were made locally at J Pratt & Sons factory on Leigh Street in Ancoats. A similar pattern can be seen in the origin of the soda bottles. Of 12 stamped bottles excavated from Loom Street, six vessels came from Manchester and three from St Helens.

Ancoats was a microcosm of Manchester, not only with its own houses and factories, but also manufacturing most of the everyday material requirements of its population, pioneering this new industrialised form of urban living.

CLEANING THE CITY: SLUM CLEARANCE AND SUBURBAN HOUSING

There is extensive archaeological evidence for the slow improvement of housing conditions at the Loom Street properties in Ancoats during the later nineteenth century, reflecting a growing awareness within the city of the problems of disease caused by overcrowded and insanitary living conditions. It was not just the building of new back-to-back and blind-back houses that caused these problems, but the conversion into multiple tenancies of older eighteenth-century housing. Along with the growth of cellar dwellings, these new houses and the conversion of older properties reflected the rising population density of Manchester, particularly during the 1820s and 1830s.

Properties such as the workshop dwellings on Angel Street, Liverpool Road and Milk Street retain physical evidence to show how older, good quality housing declined into slum dwellings occupied by multiple families. At Nos 1-5 Milk Street archaeological evidence indicates that the doorways between the loft workshops were blocked and new external stairwells added to provide separate access to the cellars. This allowed at least one family per floor of the building, so that in the 1841 Census as many as 20 people were living in a single property which once accommodated just one family. The excavations in Angel Street revealed some of the arrangements necessary to convert an eighteenth-century basement into a cellar dwelling; new access was provided by an inserted stairwell which entered from the street, whilst two rooms were created by the insertion of a one-brick-wide partition. These rooms were heated by two small inserted fireplaces.

At No. 37 Liverpool Road the changes necessitated by multiple occupancy included the building of external steps down into the cellar from Liverpool Road and the erection of a separate structure in the rear yard accessed only from Sothern's Court. Sothern's Court was reached by alleyways from Barton Street, Bridgewater Street and Southern

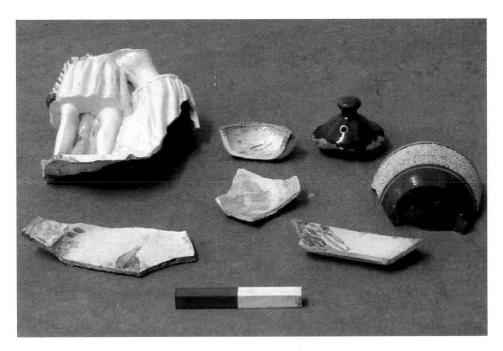

109 A typical domestic group of pottery, in this case from a pit from the back-to-back houses at the Victoria Works. A similar assemblage was recovered from several Loom Street properties

110 Soda bottles manufactured at the Hardman Street soda works. Bottles marked with the stamp from this works were excavated at Loom Street demonstrating the internal market developed in nineteenth-century Manchester

Street that ran between and behind the houses fronting these roads. Such courts grew out of building housing on the backyards of earlier properties and were a common feature of Manchester's urban landscape by the 1830s. They were a direct result of the expansion of the city in the previous half century and contained some of its most insanitary and unhealthy housing.

A consequence of this was the spread of deadly diseases in the 1830s and 1840s that threatened the functioning and existence of the new industrial city. Dr James Kay, Manchester's first Board of Health Secretary, wrote in 1832 about the 'wretched state' of houses in the vicinity of Portland Street that had courts 'a yard and a quarter wide, and contain houses, frequently three-storeys high, the lowest of which storeys is occasionally used as a receptacle of excrementitious matter' (Hylton 2003, 123). This may explain why the cellars at the Victoria Works were filled with rubbish in the mid nineteenth century. There were cholera epidemics within the city in 1832, 1849, 1854 and 1866. Several of the workers' houses excavated in recent years lie in areas affected by these outbreaks. Southern Street off Liverpool Road was in one such afflicted area in 1832, whilst Angel Street in Irk Town was badly affected in 1849. Disease outbreaks were not confined to cholera in the mid nineteenth century; tuberculosis and typhus contributed in the years 1849-51 to Manchester's annual death rate of 33 people in every thousand, well above the national average of 22 per thousand (Kidd 2002, 47-9).

The initial response of the authorities to such appalling housing conditions was slow, because local government in Manchester was weak. Prior to 1838, Manchester was governed by three bodies (Kidd 2002; Hylton 2003). The oldest was the Court Leet which had largely ceased to function by the end of the eighteenth century; next there was the Parish Vestry, and finally the Police Commissioners, established in 1792. The remit of the latter board, which was elected from a tiny minority of Manchester's population, had expanded in the early nineteenth century to include gas supply, street paving, lighting, refuse collection, the provision of a fire service and in 1831, health provision. It was not until after the new borough was formed in 1838 that local councillors began to take action to improve Manchester's health. In 1844 a local by-law was passed that stated that any new house should be equipped with a toilet, with a door and covering (Hylton 2003, 152-3). The Manchester Police Act of 1844 banned the building of new back-to-backs and allowed for them to be demolished. The building or creation of new cellar dwellings, which numbered over 5000 by the 1830s, were made illegal in 1853 by the Manchester Corporation New Streets Act. Under legislation of 1867, individual back-to-backs were declared unfit for human habitation. To bring them up to the required standard, landlords were obliged either to create a through-dwelling by knocking doors through the party wall between a pair of back-to-backs or to demolish pairs of back-to-backs or individual one-up-one-down houses to create the space for yards for the remaining property (Roberts 1999, 12-13).

Whilst all of these varying types of improvement could be detected in a number of the excavated houses at Loom Street, the archaeological and map evidence indicates that the majority of these changes were not implemented until several decades later, in the period 1888 to 1905. In Areas E and G improvements included the wholesale demolition of the early to mid nineteenth-century back-to-backs and blind-back houses, and their replacement with an outshut and then privies and yards, which were added to the late eighteenth- and mid nineteenth-century properties fronting Loom Street. It appears that a number of the blind-back and back-to-back houses were modified as part of this phase of late nineteenth-century improvement. For example, a rear room with a fireplace was added to a blind-back (House E4) fronting Loom Street, whilst the back-to-backs fronting Blossom Street were converted to through houses in the late nineteenth or early twentieth centuries. This appears to have involved the blocking of a fireplace contained within the cellar of one of the properties.

Whilst the new City Council did not itself promote the wholesale clearance of slum dwellings, it did allow new retail and commercial development in the city centre in areas of slum housing, effectively providing the same service. One of the earliest such schemes was the building of the London Road railway warehouse near Piccadilly in the 1860s that involved the demolition of 600 houses (Kidd 2002, 114). In the 1870s the construction of Central Station saw the removal of 867 workers' houses and 6070 people, and the construction of the Great Northern Railway and its warehouse in the mid 1890s necessitated the demolition of 326 houses and the eviction of 2671 tenants (Brumhead 2004).

It was the end of the nineteenth century before the city started to build its own social housing, appropriately enough in one of the worst areas of slum housing – Ancoats. The result was Victoria Square off Sherratt Street, a five-storey tenement block with an inner courtyard and balconies on four floors built for the council in 1897 (*111*). There were originally 235 two-room and 48 single-room flats, with pairs of flats sharing a communal lobby with a sink and water closet. Close by are the council properties in Anita Street (originally Sanitary Street) and George Leigh Street built around the same time. Anita Street had two rows of terraced houses designed as one- and two-roomed flats, whilst the terraces in George Leigh Street were built as three-bedroomed houses (Hartwell 2001, 287-8). It is a testament to the quality of this housing that they are still occupied and council owned.

The affect of the banning and removal of cellar dwellings and back-to-back houses in the mid nineteenth century was to reduce the population of the city centre and to force tenants to the suburbs of southern, eastern and northern Manchester (*112*). The middle classes of the city had begun to move to new suburbs in the 1790s (Kidd 2002, 144). Amongst the earliest of such areas were Ardwick, Cheetham Hill, Chorlton-on-Medlock and Hulme, though these were swamped by working class terraced housing by the mid nineteenth century. The open spaces of Ardwick Green and Grosvenor Square are almost the only elements of these early nineteenth-century middle class suburbs left, although there are a few early houses still to be seen. Amongst these was the façade of the 1831 residence of the Bellhouse family, known as Bellhouse House, in Grosvenor Square. The green open space of Ardwick Green, which once boasted a fashionable Georgian

111 The Victoria Buildings, a tenement block built in the 1890s in Ancoats, was the first council housing in the city

serpentine lake, retains several early houses. The earliest is No. 31, a three-storey brick property with a central pedimented doorway that was built in the period 1788-94. Ardwick Grove terrace is a range of two- and three-storey brick houses from *c.*1830 with classical surrounds to the doorways. A similar range of houses of the same period survives on Ardwick Green North (Hartwell, Hyde & Pevsner 2004, 360-1). Most of the surrounding area was covered in terraced housing by 1850 as the industrial suburbs of Ancoats and Chorlton-on-Medlock expanded into this area.

The process of building new working class suburbs has been highlighted by excavations on the campus of the University of Manchester, formerly in the southern part of Chorlton-on-Medlock (Arrowsmith, Gregory & Noble 2006). On the line of Tuer Street were uncovered the remains of one-up-one-down houses and a public house from

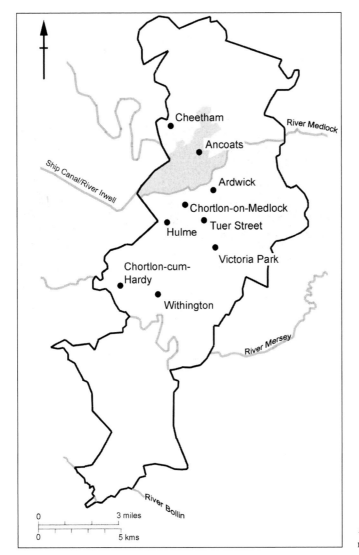

112 Manchester's
nineteenth-century suburbs

the 1820s. The map evidence shows that the township had been built up as far south as Corn Brook, which ran along the northern side of Tuer Street, by 1819. Tuer Street itself was probably laid out in the 1810s, but not paved and named until the early 1820s, as an east to west route between what was then Oxford Street in the east and Eagle Street in the west. It was probably named after a local landowner Peter Tuer who owned land on the northern side of the street as recorded in the 1841 rate book for the area. The public house, the Eagle Inn, was perhaps the earliest building in this area, being shown on a map of 1819 and was built around 1813. By 1824 it had a courtyard range of buildings to the north and according to an advertisement from that year, the licensee, one John Robson, was brewing 50 barrels a week in his own brewhouse for both the retail and wholesale market. The rate books from 1851 show that the complex included not only a brewhouse,

113 The brick barrel shoot at the Eagle Public House. This dated from the 1820s and shows how the rapidly expanding city spread southwards beyond its historic borders in this decade

but also a coachhouse and stables. It seems likely that the bowling green recorded in 1831 opposite on the southern side of Tuer Street was part of this pub complex. Given the size and early date of the public house complex it seems likely that it gave its name to the adjoining Eagle Street.

East of the inn were a row of six blind-back houses, Nos 12-24 Tuer Street, which continued to be occupied into the early twentieth century. Little of these houses survived archaeologically beyond their badly damaged half-cellars. The public house was found to be quite well preserved, with its cellars intact. These contained six rooms, one with a fireplace and another vaulted, which was probably used to store the beer barrels. It is clear that the barrels of beer from the brewhouse would have been transported across the courtyard and then rolled into a cellar via a 'barrel drop', which was found to be well-preserved when excavated (*113*).

In the south-western part of the city, Chorlton-cum-Hardy is a good example of the way in which the new rail links allowed the development of outer suburbs. It was a rural township of dispersed farmsteads in the late medieval and post-medieval periods, three miles to the south of Manchester, but by the early nineteenth century it had a small village core around Chorlton Green. When Stretford Station, at the western end of the township, opened on the Manchester South Junction and Altrincham Railway in 1849, it encouraged the building of large detached villa-style residences in Edge Lane and High Lane. Wilbraham Road was opened in 1869 and a new village centre quickly grew up where it crossed Barlow Moor Road, reinforced in 1880 by the opening of a railway station in the new village (Hartwell, Hyde & Pevsner 2004, 411). This no doubt encouraged the continued development of the area into the early twentieth century, most notably an area of semi-detached houses with wide roads and pavements, built in the years 1911-13 and known as Chorltonville.

Didsbury and, to the north, the adjacent township of Withington are two more classic southern Manchester suburbs, though their development is slightly later than Chorlton's. Horse-drawn buses reached both townships in the 1830s via Wilmslow Road, and the opening, in 1880, of railway stations in both secured their place as Manchester suburbs (Kidd 2002, 146-7). Many large detached and semi-detached villa-style houses of the mid to late nineteenth century can still be seen along Wilmslow Road, at Fielden Park and along Palatine Road. These are built in a variety of styles from Greek and Roman to Gothic and Georgian (Hartwell, Hyde & Pevsner 2004, 447-49, 486-7).

Early examples of gated communities, designed to keep the middle class in and the working class out, were Whalley Range and Victoria Park, but the latter is the best preserved and best known (Hylton 2003, 133; Kidd 2002, 145-6). Surrounded by fences and with entries guarded by toll-bars, Victoria Park in Rusholme was laid out as a planned residential suburb in 1837. The original plan, with its curving roads and crescents, remains largely intact, as do many of the nineteenth-century houses; there were 65 properties by 1850 (Parkinson-Bailey 2000, 37-8). These are a mixture of earlier Tudor-Gothic and later Baroque and Italianate detached houses. Beyond the gates, however, Rusholme was developing into a large working-class suburb characterised by two-up two-down terraced houses; in 1850 there were 431 terraced houses with more than 2000 tenants and by the time the township became part of Manchester in 1885, such housing completely surrounded Victoria Park, and the middle classes were buying detached villas in the northern Cheshire towns of Alderley Edge and Wilmslow.

EMPTYING MANCHESTER

Industrial housing (workshop dwellings, blind-backs, back-to-backs and through-houses) was a necessary counterpart to the urban, steam-powered, factory. The mill owners needed to be able to guarantee a regular supply of labour, in return for standardised wages and hours, and a new landless tenantry, in purpose-built urban houses, emerged to fulfill this need. Archaeology is now the only way of revealing the extent and quality of this housing across much of the city. The development of the Victorian middle class suburb, many of which still survive, was in part a reaction to this industrialised housing and some of its consequences, such as the prevalence of disease. In attempting to solve the worst aspects of early nineteenth-century industrial housing, the population of the centre of Manchester, its historic core, began to decline from the 1870s. The result of this was that while the population of the city as a whole grew, partly through expanding its boundaries, and reached a peak in 1931 of 766,300 people, in that same year fewer than 50,000 people were living within the city centre, whereas 130 years before in 1801 this area was home to more than 70,000 inhabitants. This trend of depopulation was encouraged by the city, culminating in the 1980s in the near total desertion of the commercial and retail heart of Manchester.

CHAPTER 7

REINVENTING MANCHESTER:
A FUTURE FOR THE CITY'S PAST

Archaeologists working in Manchester in the early twenty-first century face a dilemma. Archaeological work, whether it is excavation or building survey, is being undertaken at a greater rate than ever before, but frequently this is at the expense of the sites under study. Excavation is a destructive process and even though developments can be designed to minimise the destruction of important archaeological deposits, much of the city's past is being eroded.

The threat to historic buildings across the city is no less destructive, for even if a building is not demolished, conversion to a new use can remove features and elements which demonstrate a structure's history. Redevelopment has given archaeologists the opportunity to excavate and record elements of the city's past never studied before – from its prehistoric origins beneath Manchester Airport's second runway to the nineteenth-century glass kilns of Ancoats (*114*). Archaeological data can now contribute a vast body of new evidence concerning the development of Manchester which just 10 years ago was not available. Yet the more archaeological work that is done, the more archaeology is destroyed, and because of the way modern rescue archaeology is conducted there is now less opportunity for the public to see and actively participate in this archaeological process.

The threat of change and redevelopment has been a constant theme in the city's history. Manchester has a tradition of reinventing itself; as a medieval baronial centre, a local market place, a wool manufacturing town, a cotton spinning city, a warehouse city, a regional financial and commercial centre and as an inland port. This is one of the reasons why just a single timber-framed Tudor house, the Old Wellington, from the woollen town now survives; yet it is also why Chetham's College survives, and why archaeologists have had the opportunity to excavate medieval iron furnaces in the southern part of the city as well as prehistoric and Romano-British farmsteads within the city region.

The consequences of rapid industrialisation in the late eighteenth century and first half of the nineteenth century, and a growing awareness of the importance of the city's past, led in the later nineteenth century to the development of local government and the emergence of educational institutions, such as the Victoria University of Manchester, that would in the twentieth century help to foster the idea of investigating the past.

114 Beetham Tower, erected early in the twenty-first century, is a symbol of Manchester's prolonged building boom. It literally overshadows the eighteenth-century canal basin in Castlefield

REFORMING MANCHESTER: TWENTIETH–CENTURY ARCHAEOLOGY

In the later nineteenth century the city faced change, through the decline of the cotton spinning industry and the pressures of managing the growing industrial population. One of the consequences of this pressure was the creation of new forms of local government to manage the running of the industrial city. Manchester became a borough for the second time in 1838 and then in 1853 a city.

The visible archaeological record of the new city authority was initially small. By the 1870s there were still very few local authority buildings within the city, much of the council's energy's being spent on slum clearance and the provision of clean water. In securing a large and clean water supply, miles of brick-lined sewers were built, provision was made for waste treatment works and land in Londgendale was purchased to build an extensive water supply system. The reservoirs built from the late 1850s to the early 1870s survive and still function into the twenty-first century, as do the holding reservoirs that were built on the Gorton/Denton boundary, on the eastern side of the city.

The completion of the new town hall in 1877 began a period of local authority sponsored building whose legacy can still be seen all over the city in the early twenty-first century. These include the Corn Exchange (1897-1903) and the police and fire station on London Road (opened in 1906), whilst the city's first municipal housing was the flats built in Ancoats in 1894-9 in Victoria Square. The Manchester City Art Gallery is an example of a particular building type which began through private donation, but which was taken over by the city. Other examples of such municipalisation of building types included schools. Major buildings promoted by the City Council in the later twentieth century included the extension to the Town Hall (1934-8) (*115*), the Central Library (opened in 1934) and the Crown Court (1957-62).

The city also continued to be involved in improvements to the transport infrastructure of Manchester, which are also still reflected in the standing building record. The City Council was instrumental through its support in the building of the Manchester Ship Canal. Opened in 1894, this gave the city direct access to the sea and turned it into a deep-water harbour, leading to the city being nicknamed 'Manchester-by-the-Sea'. The Pump House is the only surviving example of a hydraulic power station for the city's extensive municipal hydraulic system developed from the 1890s to supply power for the hundreds of warehouses in Manchester (*115*). Public transport was promoted through electric trams and a fine tram depot from 1909, with art nouveau detailing and a prominent clock tower, can still be seen at the top of Princess Parkway in Moss Side. From the 1920s the City Council was also responsible for promoting motor buses; the Chorlton Street Bus Station in the centre of the city dates from the mid twentieth century. This tradition continued into the later part of the century with the city's support for the building of an inner ring road (the Mancunian Way) and an outer orbital motorway, the M60, as well as the opening of the MetroLink through the centre of the city in the early 1990s which linked the Piccadilly and Victoria stations. Through the promotion of airfields, first on the playing fields at Hough End from 1918 to 1929, then at Barton Aerodrome, which remained in council hands from 1930 to 2002 (Inglis 2004), and finally with the development of Ringway Airport from the late 1940s, the city has also provided itself with a major transport routeway to the outside world that arguably has had an even greater impact on the city and the world than the ship canal.

Such structures form the most obvious visible remains of the archaeology of the twentieth century within the city, although there are plenty of other examples – the large mid twentieth-century council housing estates in Gorton, Hulme and Wythenshawe for instance, municipal parks and gardens at Heaton Park, Platt Fields and Wythenshawe, and sports and leisure facilities such as the Firs Athletic Ground and the Victoria Baths on Hathersage Road. Yet three of the iconic symbols of twentieth-century Manchester – Trafford Park, the world's first purpose-built and planned industrial estate, the football stadium for Manchester United and Lancashire County Cricket Club's ground – lie beyond the city's formal boundaries in Stretford (*116*). These sites demonstrate that the influence of Manchester as both a cultural and commercial force continued to dominate the city region in the new century.

115 Manchester Town Hall, the most important civic building in the late nineteenth-century city and a building full of visual references to Manchester's industrial and Roman past

THE POWER OF PLACE: RECORDING AND CONSERVING MANCHESTER'S PAST

Despite the increasing pace of redevelopment in the city since 1996, the preservation, conservation and display of archaeological sites and industrial buildings has a long history in the Manchester city region which can be traced to at least the early 1970s. The emergence of an awareness of the importance and cultural value of Manchester's and the city region's past has gone through four distinct phases.

116 The pavilion at Old Trafford cricket ground in Stretford

The first phase, during the 1970s, was marked by a period of recording and listing endangered industrial buildings, coupled with the first rescue excavations. This was prompted by a period of rapid loss for many industrial structures, but in the Manchester area was particularly associated with the decline of the transport network and the closure of many of the region's early canals and railways. An early casualty was the Huddersfield Canal, closed in 1944, but the real period of neglect took hold in the early 1960s when the Ashton Canal, the Manchester, Bolton and Bury Canal, the Peak Forest Canal and the Rochdale Canal were all closed. Amongst the many railway lines and stations closed were the first railway line in the region, the Bolton and Leigh Railway, engineered by George Stephenson and opened in 1829, a year before the Manchester to Liverpool intercity line (Ashmore 1982, 104-5), and the closure of Central Station in Manchester in 1969, noted for its single span, wrought iron arched roof, only exceeded in its span by the arch at St Pancras Station in London. The most famous rescue excavation in this period was the Deansgate Dig in Manchester in 1972.

A number of industrial buildings were listed during this decade in urgent circumstances. For instance the Merchant's Warehouse, the earliest complete canal warehouse surviving within Castlefield, was given listed building status even though the roof was partially destroyed by fire in 1971 and the building subsequently lay derelict (Brumhead & Wyke 1997). Other complexes were saved by individuals or enthusiasts. Samuel Oldknow's warehouse on the Peak Forest Canal in Marple, Stockport, and dating from 1801-5, was converted into architects' offices in 1976, whilst part of the Bolton Street Station in Bury was saved by railway enthusiasts. This latter site was a passenger and goods station on the Manchester and Bolton line to Rawtenstall which had been opened in 1846. The station was closed in 1965 and most of the passenger station demolished; only the approach road, paved with stone setts, and the surrounding stone walls survived, but the goods station became the home of the Bury Transport Museum run by the East Lancashire Railway Society and was re-opened in 1972 (Ashmore 1982).

By the late 1970s, conservation in the Manchester area had moved into a second phase of piecemeal conversion and re-use of specific buildings, increasingly in urban areas, and more extensive rescue excavation work across Manchester, which was to last until the

117 The regeneration of the Liverpool Road goods station site from the mid 1970s onwards was an early catalyst for the regeneration of Manchester

early 1990s. The three biggest examples of this were the excavations of the northern gateway and interior of the Roman fort in Castlefield, the redevelopment and restoration of the Liverpool Road Railway Station, and the restoration and redevelopment of the Castlefield Basin. By the 1950s and 1960s the Castlefield area had become badly neglected due to changes in the location of city centre industries and transport routes, resulting in many rundown and abandoned buildings being demolished, canals silting and railways and viaducts becoming overgrown. In 1975 Liverpool Road Station closed and the site could have been sold for redevelopment. Fortunately in 1978 the station was bought for £1 by the Greater Manchester County Council with the intention of housing the North West Museum of Science and Industry, then residing in Grosvenor Street. The museum, now known just as the Museum of Science and Industry, opened on this site in 1983 and progressive phases of restoration have produced a large site covering several hectares and incorporating not only the 1830 passenger station, but also the 1830 railway warehouse, the 1855 transfer shed and the 1880s Lower Byrom Street Warehouse (*117*).

Since 1988 this project has run parallel with the conservation and revitalisation of the whole Castlefield area as part of the Urban Heritage Park. From 1988 until 1996 the Central Manchester Development Corporation, in partnership with Manchester City Council and others, used nearly £80 million of funds from government urban aid, the European Regional Development Fund, English Heritage, the Millennium Fund and private investment to carry out a massive programme of reconstruction and regeneration in this area (Brumhead & George

1999). Undesirable industries were relocated, dereliction removed, the Bridgewater Canal basin restored, the Merchant and Middle canal warehouses converted into flats and offices, and new canal-side housing and hotels built, along with an outdoor events arena that re-used the Staffordshire Warehouse canal arms. Other buildings converted and retained in this period included the Victoria and Albert Warehouses on Water Street and the lower lock of the Manchester and Salford Junction Canal (McNeil & George 1997). Yet the impetus for this change was the raising of public awareness directly through the action of archaeologists, in particular the work of the late Professor Barri Jones whose campaign of excavations between 1972 and 1979 not only uncovered extensive remains relating to a Roman period industrial settlement outside the Roman fort, but was responsible for a public campaign to preserve the archaeology of the whole area, both above and below ground, due to the publicity through the local media and public excavation (Jones 1984) (*118*). This campaigning activity culminated in 1979 with the designation of the Castlefield Conservation Area by the City Council. His work was continued during the 1980s by the Greater Manchester Archaeology Unit who excavated the site of two demolished canal warehouses, the Kenworthy built during the 1820s and the Staffordshire built around 1794, recorded the ruinous Merchant's canal warehouse and excavated the site

118 This 1978 reconstruction view of Roman Manchester and its vicus in the late second century was commissioned by Prof. Barri Jones. Excavations since 2001 have shown that the vicus extended further to the east and southward across the River Medlock crossing (*Image courtesy of The Manchester Museum, University of Manchester*)

of a lock keeper's cottage on the Rochdale canal, as well as investigating the Roman remains around the northern gateway of the Roman fort.

The third phase in developing this awareness for the historic landscapes of the city was very much building-focused and began in the late 1980s with the development of thematic building surveys and listing policies, allowing the examination of a large number of buildings comparatively, assessing them against criteria developed specifically for that building type (Clark 2001; English Heritage 1995a). In Manchester city region, at least, this development was spurred by a property boom, which resulted by the mid 1980s in one textile mill per week being demolished. Since it was not clear which were the most important mills, nor which were those mills that could be converted and saved, the Royal Commission on the Historical Monuments of England set up a joint mills survey with the University of Manchester in May 1985 (Williams 1988). This recorded the site of 2434 mills across the county, of which 1012 contained standing remains. Three levels of record were made for these surviving sites, the most detailed being a survey of 39 sites. Although the archive and final publication led to many mills being listed (Williams with Farnie 1992), the continued erosion of this important industrial monument type led English Heritage to undertake a further listing and upgrading exercise in the mid 1990s, resulting in the number of listed mills rising to over 80 (English Heritage 1995b; Williams 1993).

The IRA bomb of June 15 1996, besides damaging 36 listed buildings, two scheduled ancient monuments and further structures within six conservation areas (McNeil 1997), provided the opportunity to redevelop and regenerate the centre of Manchester and the city has since witnessed its longest building boom since the nineteenth century. A major beneficiary of this regeneration work was the Ancoats area. Here, the knowledge of its key industry – textiles – developed in the late 1980s and early 1990s, allowed a programme of regeneration through conservation to be undertaken, and ultimately a proposal for World Heritage Status (McNeil & George 2002). This was driven by the Ancoats Building Preservation Trust and encompassed the archaeologically led conservation of the oldest surviving cotton spinning factory in Manchester, Murray's Mill (Miller & Wild 2007). Elsewhere within the city the building boom has led to the excavation of more than 13 sites containing workers' housing and more than nine individual textile mill sites. The most prominent of these was done by *Time Team* on the Arkwright Mill site on Shudehill. Other industries have been investigated archaeologically for the first time, such as glassmaking, soda manufacture and felt hat-making. Finally, six separate investigations around the Roman fort and its associated settlement have provided new insights into the extent of the settlement and the location of its cemetery.

Nearly all of this work was undertaken as rescue archaeology through the planning process and was thus funded by the developer. A consequence of this has been the destruction of large parts of Roman and industrial Manchester (McNeil & George 2002) and the restricted access to these sites for members of the public. Yet at the same time Manchester has seen a blossoming of community archaeology projects beyond the city centre, in partnership with local communities, the University of Manchester and the City Council.

COMMUNITY ARCHAEOLOGY IN MANCHESTER

The development of community archaeology projects, that is archaeological work undertaken by local volunteers on local sites, is a feature of late twentieth- and early twenty-first-century British archaeology. In Manchester such community involvement can be traced back to the pioneering Deansgate Dig in 1972 and the outreach work of the Greater Manchester Archaeological Unit during the 1980s.

The current phase of community projects began in 2003 when a local community group in north Manchester approached the University for help in setting up a dig on the site of Moston Hall. The resultant project, Dig Moston, involved hundreds of local children, residents and disadvantaged groups and led directly to the Dig Manchester project, a city-wide community archaeology scheme that ran from 2004 to 2008. This project undertook further work at Moston Hall, as well as excavations on the site of the post-medieval cornmill at Northenden and the post-medieval farm buildings around Wythenshawe Hall (*119*). Since 2003 more than 30 schools and 8000 Manchester residents

119 A party of visitors being given a tour of the Dig Manchester community excavations at Northenden Mill in 2006. This project has allowed thousands of children and adults to participate directly in recovering the past of their city

have had the opportunity to experience the excitement of archaeological fieldwork first hand and as a consequence two new local archaeology societies have been created. Such widening participation has not only brought new community groupings together, but also has allowed archaeological sites which were not under the direct threat of redevelopment to be studied and their remains displayed.

A FUTURE FOR THE CITY'S ARCHAEOLOGY

The archaeological research of Manchester in the twentieth century laid the foundations for the early twenty-first century explosion of excavation work within the city. Inevitably, because of the way British archaeology is funded, most of this work has been undertaken as part of the planning process and as a consequence of redevelopment. However, the new insights these excavations have revealed are allowing a better appreciation of the importance of the city's past in shaping the Manchester of the early twenty-first century. The wider involvement of local communities in archaeological work provides the opportunity to spread this research across the whole city.

Manchester's story is both that of the birth of the world's first industrial city and of 34 individual communities that developed within the modern city boundaries. Whilst we know an increasing amount about how historic Manchester was formed, from its Roman foundation to the creation of the Victorian city, we know far less about the earlier farmers who lived in the surrounding landscape and who established the settlements that were the forerunners of the modern city's suburbs in places such as Blackley and Withington. Much of their history still remains hidden beneath the twenty-first century city.

GLOSSARY

ashlar – cut stone, with a very smooth surface

Blue Coat grammar school – a type of charity school maintained by voluntary contributions

borough – a self-governing town with an official charter giving it the right to elect a mayor and councillors

burgages – building plots within a medieval borough

cathead – a projecting wooden roof covering a hoist

chapel of ease – a small chapel built near a centre of population not served by its own parish church

collegiate church – a church served and administered by a group of priests often referred to as a college and supported by the income from church land

dais – a raised platform

frize – a heavy woollen fabric with a long nap

fulling – the pounding of newly woven woollen cloth in a bleaching liquid to clean and thicken the fabric

hollow way – a sunken road

intervallum – the space between the Roman fort wall and its ditch

lipids – fat residues

lithic – stone

midden – a rubbish heap

outshut – a single storey addition to a building, usually with a single-pitched roof

palaeochannel – an ancient water course

puddled clay – a water-proof lining used in canal building

revetting – shoring

sessions house – a building where the local court sat

slighting – to demolish, often associated with military sites

smallware – narrow cloths such as tapes and ribbons

Spere Truss – the side-posts of a short wooden screen projecting from a doorway, forming part of a roof truss

sunken-floored houses – Anglo-Saxon wooden houses with half-cellars

undercroft – underground chamber of vault

vicus – a Roman settlement outside a fort

zoomorphic – animal-shaped

FURTHER READING

This is not a comprehensive list of all the publications on Manchester, since there are more than a thousand historical books and papers on the city from the nineteenth and twentieth centuries alone. What follows is therefore necessarily selective, but focuses upon those publications which deal with both historic archaeological finds and excavations and more recent work, particularly since 2000. Much of the archaeological fieldwork undertaken since that date has yet to be fully published or synthesised into wider studies. However, major articles using this material are now starting to appear in the pages of the regional journals *Transactions of the Lancashire and Cheshire Antiquarian Society* and *Archaeology North West*, and the national journals *Britannia* and *Industrial Archaeology Review*.

A complete collection of the technical reports, often referred to as the 'grey literature', are held by the Greater Manchester Archaeological Unit (GMAU) and the University of Manchester Archaeological Unit (UMAU), who are both based at the University of Manchester Field Archaeology Centre. Excavation archives are held by the Manchester Museum and the Museum of Science and Industry in Manchester.

The Sites and Monuments Record/Historic Environment Record for Manchester, a database of all known archaeological and historic sites within the city, is held by the Greater Manchester Archaeology Unit. Further details on how to consult this database can be found on GMAU's website: www.arts.manchester.ac.uk/umfac/gmau.

Opportunities to become involved in exploring Manchester's past can be found through the community and outreach work of the University of Manchester Archaeology Unit, and through the activities of a number of local archaeology societies, including MADASH, the South Manchester Archaeology Research Team (SMART) and the Manchester Region Industrial Archaeology Society (MRIAS). For contact details see UMAU's website: www.arts.manchester.ac.uk/umfac/umau.

Aikin, J., 1795, *A Description of the Country Thirty to Forty Miles round Manchester*. London
Aldred, J., 1988, *Worsley, an Historical Geography*. Worsley Civic Trust
Arrowsmith, P., 1985, 'The Population of Manchester from c. AD 79 to 1801', *Greater Manchester Archaeological Journal* 1, 99-101

Arrowsmith P., Gregory R. & Noble P., 2006, *New Humanities Building: An Archaeological Investigation*. Unpublished UMAU Report 2006.39

Ashmore, O., 1982, *The Industrial Archaeology of North-West England*. Manchester University Press

Aspin, C. (ed.), 1972, *Angus Bethune Reach: Manchester and the Textile Districts in 1849*. Helmshore Local History Society, Helmshore

Aspin, C., 2003, *The Water-Spinners*. Helmshore

Axon, W.E.A. 1886, *Annals of Manchester*

Benson, A.P., 1983, *Textile Machines*. Shire Album No. 103, Shire Publications Ltd, Richborough

Bone, P.W., 2005, *A Survey of the Glass Industry in Manchester and Salford 1800-1967*. Unpublished MA Thesis, The Ironbridge Institute, University of Birmingham

Boucher, C.T., 1968, *James Brindley, Engineer, 1716-1772*. Norwich, Goose & Son Ltd

Bradshaw, L.D., 1987, *Visitors to Manchester. A Selection of British and Foreign Visitors' Descriptions of Manchester from c. 1538-1865*. Neil Richardson Publications

Brennand, M., with Chitty, G. & Nevell M. (eds), 2006, *The Archaeology of North West England. An Archaeological Research Framework for North West England: Vol 1. Resource Assessment*. (Archaeology North West Vol 8). The Association of Local Government Archaeological Officers and English Heritage with The Council for British Archaeology North West

Brumhead, D., 2004, 'Remaking the City: the impact of the railway on late Victorian Manchester', *Transactions of the Lancashire & Cheshire Antiquarian Society* 100, 135-58

Brumhead, D. & George, D., 1999, *Castlefield. A Guided Trial to Britian's First Urban Heritage Park*. Manchester Regional Industrial Archaeology Society, Manchester

Brumhead, D. & Wyke T., 1997, 'The Duke's Agents have made a wharf? Castlefield and its Warehouses', in McNeil & George 1997, 26-9

Chaloner, W.H., 1955, 'Robert Owen, Peter Drinkwater and the Early Factory System in Manchester, 1788-1800', *Bulletin of the John Rylands Library, Manchester*, Vol. 37, 78-102

Champness, B., 2004, *A History of Simpson's Mill, Shudehill, Manchester*. Manchester Region Industrial Archaeology Society

Champness, B. & Nevell, M., 2003, 'A Note on the Archaeology of Manchester's Glass Industry', *Industrial Archaeology North West*, Vol. 1.3 (Issue 3), 22-4

Chapman, S.D., 1981, 'The Arkwright Mills – Colquhoun's census of 1788 and archaeological evidence', *Industrial Archaeology Review* 6 (1), 5-27

Clark, K., 2001, *Informed Conservation. Understanding historic buildings and their landscapes for conservation*. English Heritage, London

Connelly, P., 2002, *73/83 Liverpool Road, Manchester – an archaeological excavation within the Roman Vicus*. Unpublished excavation report, the University of Manchester Archaeological Unit

Cooper, A.V., 1991, *The Manchester Commercial Textile Warehouse, 1780-1914: A Study of its Typology and Practical Development*. Unpublished PhD thesis, Manchester Polytechnic in collaboration with Manchester School of Architecture

Crowe, N., 1994, *English Heritage Book of Canals*. English Heritage and Batsford, London

Daniels, G.W., 1915, 'Valuation of Manchester Cotton Factories in the Early Years of the Nineteenth Century', *Economic Journal 25*, 625-6

Earwaker, J.P. (ed.), 1888, *The Court Leet Records of the Manor of Manchester, volume VII, From the Year 1731 to 1756*. Manchester

Engels, F., 1845, *The Conditions of the Working Class in England*. London, reprinted 1980

English Heritage, 1995a, *Industrial Archaeology: A Policy Statement*. English Heritage, London

English Heritage, 1995b, *Manchester Mills: Understanding Listing*. English Heritage, London

Farey, J., 1827, *A Treatise on the Steam Engine*. London

Fitzgerald, R., 1988, 'The Development of the Cast Iron Frame in Textile Mills to 1850', *Industrial Archaeology Review* 10 (2), 127-45

Garner, D.J., 2007, *The Neolithic and Bronze Age Settlement at Oversley Farm, Styal, Cheshire. Excavations in advance of Manchester Airport's Second Runway, 1997-8*. Gifford Archaeological Monographs Number One, Oxford

George, D. & Brumhead, D., 2002, 'The Mersey Irwell Navigation – The Old Quay at Manchester', in McNeil & George 2002, 22-24

Giles, C. & Goodall, I.H., 1992, *Yorkshire Textile Mills. The Buildings of the Yorkshire Textile Industry 1770-1930*. Royal Commission on the Historical Monuments of England, HMSO, London

George, D & Brumhead, D., 2002, 'The Mersey Irwell Navigation – The Old Quay at manchester', in McNeil, R. & George, D. (eds), *Manchester – Archetype City of the Industrial Revolution. A Proposed World Heritage Site*. The Heritage Atlas 4, University of Manchester Field Archaeology Centre

Gregory, R.A., 2005, *Hardman Street Soda works, Deansgate, Manchester*. Unpublished UMAU Report 2005. 78

Gregory, R.A., 2006, *Excavation at Barton Street, Castlefield, Manchester*. Unpublished UMAU Report 2006. 45

Gregory, R.A., 2007a, *Roman Manchester: The University of Manchester's Excavations within the Vicus 2001-5*. Oxbow Books, Oxford

Gregory, R.A., 2007b, *Loom Street, Ancoats, Manchester. An Archaeological Excavation of Late Eighteenth and Nineteenth Century Workers' Housing*. Unpublished UMAU Report 2007. 60

Greene, P., 1995, 'The 1995 Chaloner Memorial Lecture: the 1830 warehouses and the nineteenth century trade in timber', *Transactions of the Lancashire and Cheshire Antiquarian Society* Vol. 90 for 1994, 1-14

Griffiths, R.P., 1958, *The Cheshire Lines Railway*. The Oakwood Press, Salisbury

Griffiths, D., 2001, 'The North-West Frontier', in N.J. Higham & D.H. Hill (eds), 167-87

Hadfield C. & Biddle G., 1970, *The Canals of North West England*. Two volumes. The Canals of the British Isles Series, David & Charles, Newton Abbot

Hartwell, C., 2001, *Pevsner Architectural Guides. Manchester*. Penguin Books, London

Hartwell, C., Hyde, M., & Pevsner, N., 2004, *The Buildings of England. Lancashire: Manchester and the South-east*. Yale University Press, London

Higham, N.J., 2004, *A Frontier Landscape. The North West in the Middle Ages.* Windgather Press, Lancaster

Higham, N.J. & Hill, D.H. (eds), 2001, *Edward the Elder: 899-924.* London, Routledge

Hills, R.L., 1970, *Power in the Industrial Revolution.* Manchester

Hodgkins, D., 2004, 'Sir Edward Wakin: A Manchester Man and the Cheshire Lines', in *Moving Manchester. Aspects of the History of Transport in the city and region since 1700*, Brumhead, D. & Wyke, T. (eds), Lancashire & Cheshire Antiquarian Society, Manchester, 119-34

Hradil, I., Arrowsmith, P. & Nevell, M., 2007, *The Smith's Arms, Ancoats, Manchester: An Archaeological Building Survey.* Unpublished UMAU Report. 2007. 28

Hylton, S., 2003, *A History of Manchester.* Phillimore, Chichester

Inglis, S., 2004, *Played in Manchester. The architectural heritage of a city at play.* English Heritage, London

Jones, G.D.B., 1984, *Past Imperfect. A History of Rescue Archaeology.* Phillimore, Chichester

Jones, G.D. B. & Grealey, S., 1974, *Roman Manchester.* Altrincham, Manchester Excavation Committee

Jones, G.D.B. & Reynolds, P., 1978, *The Deansgate Excavations 1987 – an interim report.* Greater Manchester Council, Greater Manchester Archaeological Group, Manchester Museum & Dept of Archaeology, University of Manchester

Jones, W., 1996, *Dictionary of Industrial Archaeology.* Sutton Publishing Limited

Kenyon, D., 1991, *The Origins of Lancashire.* Manchester University Press

Kidd, A., 2002, *Manchester.* Edinburgh University Press (3rd edn).

Little, S., 2007, 'The Growth of Manchester and its Textile Industry', in Miller, I. & Wild, C. (eds), 7-24

Malet, H., 1977, *Bridgewater. The Canal Duke 1736-1803.* Manchester University Press, 99

McNeil, R., 1997, 'After the Bomb and Beyond the Arndale: the Impact of the Manchester Bomb on the City's Heritage', *Archaeology North West* Vol. 2.5 (Issue 11), 116-7

McNeil, R., 2004, 'The 1830 Railway Warehouse: an old model for a new system', *Transactions of the Lancashire & Cheshire Antiquarian Society* Vol. 100, 91-101

McNeil, R. & George, A.D. (eds), 1997, *The Heritage Atlas 3: Warehouse Album.* University of Manchester Field Archaeology Centre

McNeil, R. & George, A.D., 2002, *Manchester – Archetype City of the Industrial Revolution. A proposed World Heritage Site.* University of Manchester Field Archaeology Centre.

McNeil, R. & Nevell, M., 2000, *A Guide to the Industrial Archaeology of Greater Manchester.* Association for Industrial Archaeology

Miller, I., 2007, 'Percival Vickers & Co Ltd, Ancoats: The Archaeology of the Nineteenth-Century Manchester Flint Glassworks', *Industrial Archaeology Review* 29 (I), 13-29

Miller, I. & Wild, C., 2007, *A & G Murray and the Cotton Mills of Ancoats.* Lancaster Imprints 13, Oxford Archaeology North, Lancaster

Morris, M. (ed.), 1983, *Medieval Manchester: A Regional Study.* The Archaeology of Greater Manchester Vol. I

Musson, A.E., 1973, 'Engineering', in Smith, J.H. (ed.), *The Great Human Exploit. Historic Industries of the North West.* University of Manchester Dept of Extra Mural Studies, 55-61

Musson, A.R. & Robinson, E., 1969, *Science and Technology in the Industrial Revolution.* Manchester

Nevell, M., 1994, 'Rainsough: A Romano-British Site in the Irwell Valley', *Archaeology North-West* 7, 11-5

Nevell, M., 1997, *The Archaeology of Trafford. A Study of the Origins of Community in North West England Before 1900.* Greater Manchester Archaeological Unit, University of Manchester Archaeological Unit and Trafford Metropolitan Borough

Nevell, M. (ed.), 1999, *Living on the Edge of Empire: Models, Methodology & Marginality. Late-Prehistoric and Romano-British Rural Settlement in North-West England.* CBA North West, the Field Archaeology Centre at the University of Manchester and Chester Archaeology

Nevell, M., 2003, 'From Linen Weaver to Cotton Manufacturer: Manchester during the 17th and 18th centuries and the social archaeology of industrialisation', in Nevell, M. (ed.), *From Farmer to Factory Owner. Models, Methodology and Industrialisation. Archaeological Approaches to the Industrial Revolution in North West England.* CBA North West & CBA North West Industrial Archaeology Panel

Nevell, M., 2004, 'The River Irwell and the archaeology of Manchester's early waterfronts', *Transactions of the Lancashire & Cheshire Antiquarian Society* Vol. 100, 30-50

Nevell, M., 2005, 'The Social Archaeology of Industrialisation: The Example of Manchester during the 17th and 18th Centuries', in Casella, E.C. & Symonds, J., *Industrial Archaeology. Future Directions.* Springer New York, 177-204

Nevell, M., Connelly, P., Hradil, I. & Stockley, S., 2003, 'The Archaeology of the Textile Finishing Trades in North West England', in Nevell, M. (ed.), *From Farmer to Factory Owner. Models, Methodology and Industrialisation. Archaeological Approaches to the Industrial Revolution in North West England.* CBA North West & CBA North West Industrial Archaeology Panel

Nevell, M. & Hradil, I., 2005a, *The Archaeology of Tameside Volume 4: St Lawrence's Church, Denton, and the Archaeology of the Timber-framed Churches of North West England.* Tameside MBC and University of Manchester Archaeological Unit

Nevell, M. & Hradil, I., 2005b, *The Archaeology of Tameside Volume 5: The Two Saint Michaels and the Archaeology of the Medieval Parish Church in North West England.* Tameside MBC and University of Manchester Archaeological Unit

Nevell, M. & Redhead, N. (ed.), 2005, *Mellor: Living on the Edge. A Regional Study of an Iron Age and Romano-British Upland Settlement.* Manchester Archaeological Monographs Vol. 1, University of Manchester Field Archaeology Centre

Nevell, M., & Walker, J.S.F., 1998, *A History and Archaeology of Tameside. Volume 6. Lands and Lordships in Tameside: Tameside in Transition 1348-1642.* Tameside Metropolitan Borough Council with the University of Manchester Archaeological Unit

Nevell, M. & Walker, J.S.F., 2001, *Portland Basin and the Archaeology of the Canal Warehouse.* Tameside Metropolitan Borough with the University of Manchester Archaeological Unit

Nevell, M. & Walker, J.S.F., 2002, *Denton and Dukinfield Halls and the Archaeology of the Gentry and Yeoman House in North West England 1500 to 1700.* Vol. 2, Archaeology of Tameside Series, Tameside MBC and University of Manchester Archaeological Unit

Nevell, M. with Grimsditch, B. & Hradil, I., 2007, *Denton and the Archaeology of the Felt Hatting Industry.* Vol. 7, Archaeology of Tameside Series; Tameside MBC and University of Manchester Archaeological Unit

Ogden, J., 1783, *A Description of Manchester by a Native of the Town.* Manchester, reprinted 1883

Palmer, M. & Neverson, P., 1998, *Industrial Archaeology, Principles and Practice.* Routledge, London & New York

Parkinson-Bailey, J.J., 2000, *Manchester. An Architectural History.* Manchester University Press

Petch, J.A., 1950-1, 'The northern defences of Roman Manchester', *Transactions of the Lancashire & Cheshire Antiquarian Society 62,* 177-96

Petch, J.A., 1956, 'The foundations of the north gateway of Roman Manchester', *Transactions of the Lancashire & Cheshire Antiquarian Society 66,* 29-37

Phelps, J.J., 1912, 'The north wall of the Roman fort at Manchester', *Transactions of the Lancashire & Cheshire Antiquarian Society 30,* 195-225

Phillips, C.B. & Smith, J.H., 1994, *A Regional History of England: Lancashire and Cheshire from AD 1540.* Longman, London and New York

Prince H.C., 1973, 'England circa 1800', in Darby , H.C. (ed.) *A New Historical Geography of England.* Cambridge University Press, 389-464

Raffald, E., 1773, *Directory of Manchester and Salford.* Manchester, reprinted 1889

Redhead, N., 1996, 'Medieval Furnaces in the Castleshaw Valley', *Archaeology North West* Vol. 2.4 (Issue No. 10), 99-104

Redhead, N., 2004, 'The Archaeology of South-East Lancashire', in Hartwell, Hyde & Pevsner 2004, 11-22

Roberts, J., 1993, 'The Residential Development of Ancoats', *Manchester Region History Review VII,* 15-26

Roberts, J., 1997, 'From Warehouse to Town House: some small warehouses of the 18th and 19th centuries', in McNeil & George 1997, 15-16

Roberts, J., 1999, *Working Class Housing in Nineteenth Century Manchester. John Street, Irk Town, 1826-1936.* Neil Richardson Publications, Radcliffe, 2nd ed.

Roeder, C., 1899, 'Recent Roman discoveries in Deansgate and on Hunt's bank and Roman Manchester restudied', *Transactions of the Lancashire & Cheshire Antiquarian Society* 17

Roeder, C., 1906, 'Additional notes on the beginnings of Manchester', *Transactions of the Lancashire & Cheshire Antiquarian Society 24,* 173-9

Rose, R.E., 1987, *The LMS & LNER in Manchester.* Ian Alan Ltd, London

Rush, R.W., 1983, *The East Lancashire Railway.* The Oakwood Press, Salisbury

Sanders, G., 1991, 'Walker's Buildings, Manchester. An Investigation of 19th Century Workers' Housing', *Archaeology North West* Vol. 1.2, 8-10

Savage, A. (ed.), 1982, *The Anglo-Saxon Chronicles.* Phoebe Phillips & Heinemann, London

Stobart, J., 1998, 'Textile Industries in north-west England in the Early Eighteenth Century: A Geographical Approach', *Textile History* 29, 3-18

Tann, J., 1979, 'Arkwright's employment of steam power: a note of some new evidence', *Business History* XXI

Taylor, S., Cooper, M. & Barnwell, P.S., 2002, *Manchester. The Warehouse Legacy. An Introduction and Guide.* English Heritage, London

Thompson, W.H., n.d., *The Byroms of Manchester.* 3 vols, privately published, Manchester Central Library

Timmins, G., 1998, *Made in Lancashire. A history of regional industrialisation.* Manchester University Press

Tindall, A., 1983, 'Investigations at Chetham's School, Manchester', *Greater Manchester Archaeological Unit Annual Report 1982-83*, 5-8

Tomlinson, V.I., 1961, 'Early warehouses on Manchester waterways', *Transactions of the Lancashire & Cheshire Antiquarian Society* 71, 129-51

Wadsworth, A.P. & Mann, J. de Lacy, 1931, *The Cotton Trade and Industrial Lancashire 1600-1780.* Manchester University Press

Walker, J.S.F. (ed.), 1986, *Roman Manchester: A Frontier Settlement.* The Archaeology of Greater Manchester, Vol. 3, Greater Manchester Archaeological Unit

Walker, J.S.F. (ed.), 1989. *Castleshaw – The Archaeology of a Roman Fortlet.* The Archaeology of Greater Manchester, Vol. 4, Greater Manchester Archaeological Unit

Whitaker J., 1773, *History of Manchester*, Vol. 2. Manchester

Willan, T.S., 1979, 'Manchester Clothiers in the Early Seventeenth Century', *Textile History* 10, 175-183

Willan, T.S., 1980, *Elizabethan Manchester.* MUP

Willan, T.S., 1983, 'Plague in perspective: the case of Manchester in 1605', in Kermode J.I. & Phillips, C.B. (eds), *Seventeenth-Century Lancashire. Essays Presented to J J Bagley.* Transactions of the Lancashire & Cheshire Antiquarian Society Vol. 132

Williams, M., 1988, 'The RCHME/GMAU Joint Survey of Textile Mills in Greater Manchester', *Industrial Archaeology Review* X, 193-203

Williams, M., 1993, 'Havelock Mill, Manchester: a case-study in the emergency recording of a large urban mill complex', *Industrial Archaeology Review* XVI, 100-10

Williams, M. with Farnie, D., 1992, *Cotton Mills in Greater Manchester*, The Greater Manchester Archaeological Unit in association with the Royal Commission on the Historical Monuments of England, Carnegie Publishing Ltd, Preston

Winterbottom, D., 1998, '"Sackclothes and fustyans and such like com'odyties". Early linen manufacture in the Manchester region', in Roberts E. (ed.), *A History of Linen in the North West.* Centre for North-west Regional Studies, University of Manchester, 22-43

INDEX